To My Favorite
Conservationist

Best,

Tod

REACHING BEYOND RACE

REACHING BEYOND RACE

PAUL M. SNIDERMAN

EDWARD G. CARMINES

HARVARD UNIVERSITY PRESS
Cambridge, Massachusetts
London, England
1997

Library of Congress Cataloging-in-Publication Data

Sniderman, Paul M.
Reaching beyond race /
Paul M. Sniderman, Edward G. Carmines
p. cm.
Includes bibliographical references and index.
ISBN 0-674-14578-X
1. United States—Race relations—Public opinion.
2. Afro-Americans—Civil rights—Public opinion.
3. Whites—United States—Attitudes.
4. Racism—Political aspects—United States.
5. United States—Politics and government—1993–
6. Public opinion—United States.
I. Carmines, Edward G.   II. Title.
E185.615.S5854   1997
305.8′00973—dc21   97-14658

For
Jennifer, Mark, and Suzie
and
Paige and Ethel

PREFACE

This is a book about what white Americans think about race—
what they really think and not just what they think they
should say. According to the standard view, the primary barrier
to a new effort to assist badly off Americans, white and black,
is the resistance of white Americans. Without minimizing this
barrier, we show that the deeper problem is political leadership. Our empirical results show that it is possible—not a sure
thing, but not out of the question either—to win the support
of a coalition of white and black Americans in behalf of policies to assist the badly off, both black and white, provided that
political leaders base their appeal on moral principles that
reach beyond race.

Specifically, we shall argue for three propositions: that the
only way to break through the current impasse over race is to
re-form a coalition of black and white Americans; that a winning biracial coalition can only be re-formed on the basis of
principles that both black Americans and white Americans are
committed to; and that since citizens only get to choose from
among the choices on offer, the only way that ordinary Americans, whether black or white, can show their support for a
policy based on these shared principles is if political leaders
appeal for their support on the right grounds.

There is, of course, a fog of skepticism that hangs over public opinion surveys on sensitive issues like race. Surely people will not be candid. They will understate their prejudices; they will overstate their fairmindedness. The problem of candor is genuine. To come to grips with it, we have developed a new approach to the study of public opinion. Taking advantage of computer-assisted interviewing, we hide experiments in an apparently ordinary public opinion interview. These experiments take different forms, but each is designed to persuade the people we talk to that they can express how they really feel about matters of race without the risk of appearing racist. It is for others, when they have had the opportunity to examine our results, to judge how far we have succeeded. Certainly, no measurement procedure is perfect. But having cross-checked our findings as closely as we can, we believe this new approach throws light on aspects of white Americans' thinking about race hitherto hidden.

In the course of carrying out this study, our empirical findings collided with our personal presuppositions. White Americans, we had supposed, had first to be won over to racial tolerance for racial progress to be possible. What we saw for the first time, taking advantage of our hidden experiments, is that the support of whites could be won for a new effort to help those who are badly off, blacks as well as whites, *just as things stand*. But their support can be won only by appealing to moral principles that reach beyond race.

Thoughtful people, we recognize, contend that there cannot be a color-blind politics in a society that continues to be color-conscious. Since the issue is complex, in addition to being controversial, we want to state our view clearly: To win the support of a large enough number of Americans in behalf of a new initiative to relieve poverty and immiseration, it is necessary to give them more than a good reason. It is necessary to give them the best reason possible. This does not mean ignoring the moral character of race as an issue in American life. It does mean remembering what we once knew. The strongest arguments in behalf of equality for black Americans reach beyond race to the moral principles to which both black and white Americans are committed, not as blacks or whites, but as Americans. For they are, in the end, the principles that give the issue of race itself a moral claim upon us.

CONTENTS

FIGURES, TABLES, AND APPENDIXES

Figures

Tables

Appendixes

CHAPTER ONE

■

TANGLED POLITICS

Race was once supposed to be an issue we would put behind us. Progress would be difficult, conflict protracted, short-term set-backs inevitable, struggles on many fronts necessary. Certainly a formal guarantee of equality under the law for black Americans was only a beginning. But America was steadily becoming a more open and open-minded society, as increasingly better-educated and more tolerant Americans took the place of ill-educated and intolerant ones. With time, it was said, the rancor and bitterness over race would abate.

But race has not receded into the background of American life. On the contrary, gaping cleavages are obvious, not just at the margins of American society but at its center, in its institutions of government and advanced education. As every person of prominence in American thought and politics recognizes, race remains as divisive as ever. Why, more than a quarter of a century after the landmark civil rights laws of the 1960s, does the issue of race still cut so deep?

Many believe that the continuing clash over race is rooted ultimately in the persistent reluctance of white Americans to accept black Americans as equals—that is, in prejudice. Granted, this idea has not always been given the careful exposition it deserves: it is easy to point to a parade of commentators and social scientists who have made extreme and crude assertions about the continuing power of racial prejudice in

American life. But a truth should not be denied just because it has been overstated. Recognition of prejudice's pervasiveness in the American experience represents a hard-won accomplishment of the civil rights movement, and for a generation now educated and public-spirited Americans have found it next to impossible to understand the issue of race in other than moral terms. Furthermore, agreement that a historic wrong had been done to blacks, it was believed, would prove a decisive political force in itself, assuring that the public action required to achieve racial equality would in the end be taken.

But in a way that no one anticipated a generation ago, what ought to be done to achieve equality has proven politically controversial, even morally problematic. Meanwhile, the objective conditions of life of large numbers of blacks have gotten worse, also in a way that no one foresaw. Today, black Americans remain significantly more likely than whites to be poor, to be raised by a single parent, to be segregated residentially and educationally, and to die young.[1] Although more blacks are better off than ever before, a frighteningly large number are immiserated: ill-educated, ill-housed, and underemployed or unemployed.

In consequence, in the minds of many Americans, both black and white, the issue of race is now defined by an ominous trinity: the worsening of inequality as a social fact; the deepening of whites' resistance to governmental action to overcome it; and the hypocrisy of their commitment to racial equality in principle but not in public policy. For many who are most sympathetic to the problems of blacks, the very meaning of the issue of race has been transformed. Instead of testifying to the moral power of the American values of fairness and equal opportunity, race has exposed the futility of the American Creed. In place of optimism and pride, there is now resentment and bitterness. The small steps toward racial equality that have been taken only underscore the great distance that remains.

Other Americans have come to see the issue of race from a

very different perspective, however. As they view it, the intensity of the continuing clash over race owes less to the tenacity of racial prejudice and more to the very efforts undertaken to overcome it. In the name of achieving racial equality and tolerance, they contend, the ideals of equality and tolerance have themselves been upended. No shortage of self-serving acts have been defended as morally commendable, under the shield of civil rights. Especially egregious examples—say, the Tawana Brawley case or the defense of black anti-Semites— have provided a larger context in which more problematic ones—say, racially gerrymandering voting districts—are now set. In surveying the contemporary politics of race from this second perspective, it is, again, easy to focus on the failings of individual personalities engaged in the debate, but so narrow a view would miss the deeper concern: that in the effort to put right a terrible wrong, we have committed ourselves to policies that many find wrong in themselves.

A very large part of the contemporary argument over race seems to consist in a debate between these two views, the one emphasizing the tenacity of racial prejudice, the other stressing the polarizing effects of our efforts to overcome it. Although some conservatives are concerned about the persistence of prejudice, this worry is more common among those with a broadly liberal view; and although, increasingly, some liberals are expressing apprehension about the polarizing impact of government policies on race, this criticism is more common among those with a broadly conservative view.

Partly because of this convergence between ideological outlook and critical orientation, the currents that charge the contemporary debate over race are powerful and deep. Among those concerned about prejudice, many see the criticisms of public policies designed to move blacks forward as being themselves an added layer of racial prejudice, more subtle than old-fashioned bigotry but just as noxious. On the other hand, many of those who emphasize the polarizing consequences of racial policies see these claims of prejudice as a ploy to defend acts by both individuals and governments which are otherwise morally indefensible.

Obviously, one can simultaneously agree with both sides in the debate; the truth of the one does not establish the falsity of the other. But it is very far from clear how to put these two perspectives together coherently. They seem to point to two fundamentally opposed attitudes toward the American experience itself. The emphasis on the continuing power of prejudice is, and is meant to be, critical; the focus on the polarizing effects of racial policies is, and is meant to be, exculpatory.

We, the authors of this book, have thought about what is going on and why for some time, and we report here what we have discovered. Our findings rest on a fundamental claim: that the current clash over race must be interpreted in the context of a deeper debate on the proper role of government. In saying this, we are very far from suggesting that either racial prejudice or racial polarization are not genuine problems. But we are persuaded that it is not possible to understand either without understanding that the contemporary debate over racial policy is driven primarily by conflict over what government should try to do, and only secondarily over what it should try to do *for blacks*.

■ ■ ■

Liberalism has made an exceptional commitment in behalf of racial equality, transforming the politics of race, and it has made this commitment out of moral conviction. But in seeking to do the right thing, and perhaps especially in wishing to do it for the right reason, there are great risks as well as great rewards.

A call for a national undertaking to bring to an end the legal segregation of black Americans, and to work actively to overcome the legacy of slavery and discrimination, had a natural appeal to liberals. The values of liberalism—the commitment to equality, belief in the efficacy of government as a agent of social change, openness to change, and concern for the less well-off—combined to serve as a foundation for a collective effort to improve the conditions of life for blacks. This is not to say that conservatives were opposed, on principle, to a national struggle for racial equality: and, on an individual level, large numbers of conservatives did support the struggle for civil rights. But a deliberate and public effort at social change in behalf of the disadvantaged, through the medium of the national government, had an indisputably stronger appeal for liberals. Liberalism has, in consequence, been the dominating political force that has energized and directed the campaign for civil liberties and civil rights of black Americans.

Viewed from the perspective of traditional American liberalism, the politics of race has centered on the resistance of white Americans to public policies designed to achieve racial equality. The reasons for white resistance are variously conceived. Some believe that the root of opposition is racial prejudice pure and simple. Others believe that the obstacle is the American value of individualism, or perhaps the American vice of self-interestedness. Still others see the problem as group interest, that is, whites acting in the interest of whites whether it is in their individual interest or not. But whether they believe that opposition to policies designed to achieve racial equality is rooted in opposition to racial equality itself or in some other factor, traditional liberals agree that the resistance of whites is the principal barrier to achieving racial equality. The problem of race, now as ever, is defined by them as a problem in the hearts and minds of white Americans.

From this view of the racial problem a political strategy followed: in order to improve the conditions of life for blacks, it is first necessary to change the beliefs and sentiments of ordinary white Americans—above all, to beat back the racial prejudice and resentment that was preventing blacks from achieving equality. Over time, almost imperceptibly, seeing blacks better off became itself the animating objective of liberalism, the goal liberals sought even when it was at odds with liberal values, tolerance and the moral irrelevance of race among them. Liberals thus came to evaluate racial policies increasingly in the light of their fundamental desire to see blacks better off, and only secondarily in light of the constitutive values of liberalism itself. And precisely because of the sincerity of liberalism's moral commitment to overcoming racial inequality, politically engaged liberals found themselves, at least in the early years, disposed to make use of the coercive power of government to a degree they would ordinarily abhor. Many still see the benefits to be gained from the determined use of public power in programs like busing or affirmative action, and indeed some believe that if a mistake has been made it has been to underuse, not overuse, the authority of government to promote racial equality and oppose the resistance of whites.[2] Many liberals are committed to staying the course.

But alongside these traditional liberals now are many other liberals who believe that liberalism itself has taken a wrong turn. Their objection is not to the cost of government in alleviating inequality, nor is it even to the use of government power to promote equality, at any rate not in the abstract. The difficulty instead is moral. The campaign for racial equality, which they support as liberals, has come to serve ends to which they object *as liberals*. Programs dedicated to equal opportunity, as a practical matter, have condoned unequal treatment under the law, in the form of race-conscious policies, just as the effort to promote racial tolerance on college campuses by imposing "hate speech" codes has come to seem at odds with freedom of expression itself. The result is that, quite apart from having to wrestle with conservatism, liberalism is now engaged in a struggle with itself.

■ ■ ■

For many years, we intuitively believed, along with many traditional liberals, that racial prejudice, pure and simple, still shaped the political thinking of white Americans. At the start of our studies of public opinion, we, like everyone else, wanted to address the question: To what extent does racial prejudice persist? It is manifestly important to answer this question, and in the chapters that follow we shall present much in the way of new evidence bearing on it. For example, we will describe the surprising finding—surprising to us certainly—that although prejudice is more common on the political right, it is more powerful on the left, among liberals themselves. Still, judged by the objective evidence, the overall impact of racial prejudice on the political choices that white Americans make turns out to be surprisingly modest. We first discovered this when examining our own surveys of American racial attitudes; then we corroborated it, analyzing every other survey available. The conclusion to draw now is clear: racial prejudice is not the dominant reason for the resistance of white Americans to current policies intended to help black Americans.

But there is another question, equally important to answer. As the story of race has been told, it has focused on whether racial prejudice has declined. Some argue that a real change has taken place, others that the changes have been superficial. But with all the debate over whether the decline in prejudice has been large or small, another change has escaped attention. Not only has there been a decrease in the number of whites who harbor ill will toward blacks, but there has also been an increase in the number of whites who bear good will toward them—indeed, so much so that there are now two forces at work, not just one: a weakening strain of animosity *and* a strengthening desire that, at last, blacks be better off. To fail to see that, now, at least as large a number of whites genuinely wish blacks well as wish them ill is to fail to see the possibilities for positive political action.

Whether this new well-spring of good will is put to use, and, no less important, what use it is put to, depends upon the choices that political leaders offer to the public at large and the arguments they make in their behalf. The results we have uncovered and present in this book suggest a strategy for achieving racial equality that is quite different from the now conventional liberal approach. It is *not* necessary to change the hearts and minds of white Americans to win support for public policies that make things go better for blacks.[3] It is instead necessary to change the terms on which political leaders appeal for support. Public support can be won, provided political leaders appeal directly to the moral principles that give the issue of race itself a moral claim upon us.

Our findings suggest that the very same policies meant to reach out and help those most in need of help will win markedly more public support if they are championed on the basis of universal principles that reach beyond race instead of being justified on racially specific grounds. The advantage of a color-blind politics is not that it wins the support of whites who would otherwise object to programs to help blacks, whether out of racial prejudice or self-interestedness. Reaching beyond race has a power to it, not because it evades the reach of prejudice but because it calls into play the principle of fairness—that all who need help should be helped, regardless of their race.

An appeal to fairness or compassion without a special focus on race is interpreted by some liberals as an effort to undercut special claims that blacks may make for government assistance. They argue that because blacks have been forced to bear unique burdens, they are entitled to make unique claims. The effect is to cast racial politics as a form of reparation. But this view of racial politics confuses two different questions: Who should be helped and why they should be helped? A policy may focus on helping blacks. But that does not mean it must be argued for on racial grounds. Indeed, the most effective way to argue on behalf of blacks, as we shall show, is to argue on grounds that do not apply exclusively to blacks.

If political leaders will move from arguments restricted to considerations of racial justice to arguments centered on

broader considerations of social justice, they can build a biracial coalition in support of policies to assist those in need of
assistance regardless of race. Political leaders are themselves
constrained by public opinion, but the choices we make as
citizens depend on the choices they make as leaders. They not
only establish the alternatives but also fix the justifications for
alternative courses of action. Political leaders thus define both
the lines of government action that citizens may choose to
support or oppose, and the reasons why they should do one
rather than the other.

In saying this, we are not saying that public opinion can
easily be swayed or that majorities can be conjured up out of
minorities on issues of race simply by cunningly framing the
issues in one way rather than other. Bringing about a change
in the center of gravity of public opinion, on issues that are inescapably controversial, is inherently difficult. But it is doable.
And what seems to us so unfortunate about the longstanding
fixation with the malignant strain in American popular culture
is the impression of fixity that it gives to the politics of race.
It suggests that intolerance remains the primary factor shaping
public reactions to matters of race and that, unless and until
it is eliminated—an event which appears nowhere on the ho-
rizon—political leaders who engage problems of race face a
huge risk of provoking resentment and a vanishingly small
chance of winning public support.

If this view of the hegemony of racial prejudice and resentment is accurate, political leaders have little to gain from
attempting to move the discussion of race forward: they will
earn plaudits from a few; they will suffer censure from many.
It is our deep belief that this view is wrong. The all-too-com-
mon tendency to cast the politics of race as a clash between
two nations, one white, the other black, obscures what is most
crucial to the politics of race—namely that whites do not form
a singleminded nation. On the contrary, there is a real division among whites over race. Approximately as many support

many policies to help blacks as oppose them, and still others can be won from one side to the other. Moreover, to change the minds of those whose minds are open to change does not require that their core ideas about race be altered. It does require that political leaders, both in public office and out of it, change the moral arguments they make to them as to what should be done about race and why.

But change their minds about what? A generation ago, in a fundamental sense there was only one question to decide. If you believed that it was wrong to forbid blacks from drinking from the same water fountain as whites, it followed that it was wrong to forbid them to attend the same schools as whites. If segregation was wrong in one situation, it was wrong in all situations. Now, there is more than one question to decide.[4] If you believe that government should help blacks in some ways, it does not follow that it ought to help them in all ways.

More than one decision now needs to be made about racial policy. Our aim, accordingly, is to establish how ordinary Americans believe these different decisions, some involving race-conscious policies and some not, should be made. In the chapters that follow we map public opinion about an array of proposals for public action, among them to boost black employment, to improve public education, to provide job training programs, to combat discrimination in employment and housing, to reduce poverty. With the exception of affirmative action—understood as requiring preferential treatment or racial quotas—all are politically contestable. On each of these issues large numbers are wedded to their positions, but substantial numbers are not. They can be won from one side to the other—from opposing government assistance for blacks to supporting it, or from supporting it to opposing it, or indeed from sitting on the sidelines to taking a stand.

To sum up our view of the politics of race, we believe (1) that there is not one problem of race but a number of distinguishable problems calling for different courses of action; (2) that to talk of a solution to the issue of race is misleading, not only because there is more than one problem of race to deal with but also because no one has a credible plan for the complete solution of any of the fundamental problems; (3) that it is essential, as both a moral and practical matter, to establish priorities, and although middle-class blacks are not yet as well off as middle-class whites, they are now decisively better off than poor blacks and poor whites; it follows, in our view, that those who are badly off should be given priority over members of the middle-class, regardless of race; (4) that any effort to help those who are badly off will require increased public efforts to improve their opportunities for education and employment; (5) that winning public support for such efforts will require a coalition of blacks and whites, working together on the basis of values they believe in by virtue not of being black or white but of being American; and (6) that continuing to reduce the complexities of race to a morality play dividing the right thinking and racially tolerant on the one side from the intolerant and self-interested on the other will sink constructive efforts to relieve the real and persisting problems of race for another generation.

We shall assume the first four points and, in the chapters that follow, demonstrate the last two.

■　■　■

But is it possible to establish what white Americans really think about matters of race? A generation ago, it seemed self-evident that the way to find out what citizens thought on the issues of the day was to conduct a systematic survey of public opinion. Since then, cynicism has set in on the value of public opinion polls, perhaps especially on matters of race. Can we learn, by means of opinion surveys, not what white Americans think they should say but what they really think? Can we establish whether, if they say they wish blacks to be treated fairly, they mean what they say? One does not have to be a cynic to be skeptical about what people say in public opinion interviews. Race is still an emotionally charged issue, difficult to discuss with friends, harder still with strangers.

Given the manifest difficulty of determining whether people mean what they say when they talk about race, it is ironic that so many popular commentators are so sure that they really know what the ordinary white American thinks about blacks. Even when politically committed commentators are aware of the carefully compiled record of public opinion surveys since the 1940s showing a dramatic decline in levels of racial prejudice among whites, they nonetheless point out that some whites are not telling the truth about how they feel about blacks. But, from a valid premise—that one cannot be certain that everyone is telling the truth—they draw an invalid conclusion—that one can be confident that large numbers of them are not telling the truth. The result: some of the best-known commentators contend that racial prejudice, rather than being in decline, remains pervasive.[5] Yet they do not themselves present reliable evidence of what even a small number of white Americans actually think. So skepticism, with the assistance of self-righteousness, passes into cynicism.

For more than a decade, we have been developing a new approach to public opinion interviews which allows us to illuminate aspects of Americans' thinking about race hitherto hidden. The key to this approach is to embed complex, genuinely randomized experiments in public opinion interviews and carry them out in a way that is invisible to the person being interviewed.[6] The experiments we have developed, which rely on computer-assisted interviewing, take many different forms. Here we will briefly describe one, in order to illustrate the new light this approach can throw on American racial attitudes.

We call this group of experiments the Excuse Experiments, and the idea behind them is to create a situation in which a randomly selected set of white interviewees who say they think well of blacks are deliberately given a socially acceptable excuse to make a negative judgment of blacks, precisely in order to see if they take advantage of it. Suppose—for the moment setting aside the mechanics of how this is to be done—that a mother on welfare is characterized as a high school dropout one half of the time and as a high school graduate the other half. Suppose, moreover, that she is black one half of the time and white the other half. Then ask everyone whether they think the welfare mother they were asked about is likely to make an honest effort to get off welfare in the next year.

Imagine how whites who said they like blacks but really don't would answer when the mother was black and a high school dropout. Just so far as they think ill of blacks, even though they say they think well of them, they should be inclined to say that a black mother who is a high school dropout is unlikely to make an honest effort to get off welfare in the next year. That is what they are free to say, if that is what they think, because we have deliberately put them in a position to claim that the mother on welfare was unlikely to try to find a real job not because she is black but because she is a high school dropout. However, by seeing if their confidence is similarly undercut in the case of a white woman on welfare, we can tease out the proportion of whites who really are prejudiced without their being able to tell that we can tell. For if it turns out that being a high school dropout is more stigmatizing if the woman on welfare is black rather than white, then that difference is a proof of racial prejudice among whites who profess to think well of blacks.

The Excuse Experiments are only one group of many experiments that we will describe in this book. These new interviewing procedures make visible aspects of Americans' thinking about matters of race previously invisible. We are not suggesting that the truth about American racial attitudes now can be established completely and decisively, or that older procedures were without value. Every procedure, new or old, is imperfect, and all procedures, perhaps especially if they are new, can be improved. We do, however, believe that because of its novel approach, our study can address questions that thoughtful people have asked about the validity of public opinion polls on matters of race in a way that previous studies have not been able to do.

CHAPTER TWO

■

AFFIRMATIVE ACTION'S VORTEX

Why is the issue of race, more than a quarter of a century after the landmark civil rights laws of the 1960s, still so bitter, so festering a sore? Part of the answer has to do with affirmative action.

A firestorm of argument is raging around affirmative action. Sometimes it is asserted that opposition to affirmative action is, in and of itself, racial bigotry; sometimes, that such opposition is fueled by racial prejudice, among other factors. The first charge is polemical, but the second is serious.[1] Surely it is only reasonable to expect that the more whites dislike blacks, the more likely they are to reject affirmative action as unfair and unwarranted—indeed, the more likely they are to reject government assistance of any kind for blacks as unwarranted, whether or not they think it is unfair. The first question we want to ask, then, is:

To what extent is opposition to affirmative action driven by racial prejudice?

Racism is not the only issue, however. From the point of view of those appalled at the American history of racial discrimination and exploitation, anger over racial quotas and preferential treatment reveals, if not actual racism, then at the very least the continuing obtuseness and indifference of white

Americans to the special cross of discrimination and economic disadvantage that black Americans still must bear. Viewed from this perspective, it is not completely a coincidence that the call for a color-blind society went up just as the special problems of blacks started to receive focused attention. Consciously or not, and highminded or not, contemporary appeals for a color-blind society represent a desire to turn the clock back; to deny the special standing of race as a moral issue; to insist that badly off blacks have to move from the front of the line and take their turn like everyone else.[2]

Notice that, in this view of the problem, the issue is not the animosity that white Americans may or may not bear toward black Americans, nor even the insincerity that may or may not afflict whites when they speak of equal opportunity for blacks. The issue is rather the unwillingness of white Americans to recognize and respect the unique cruelty of the actual conditions of life that black Americans face. A second question we want to ask, then, is:

> To what extent does opposition to affirmative action mean rejection of the unique claims that black Americans are entitled to make because of the unique burdens they have borne?

It is also argued that the furor over "group rights" is fueled by a distinctively American commitment to individualism as a value.[3] The idea of individualism often covers a catch-all of concerns, sometimes including the importance of hard work and discipline, but it almost always includes opposition to government intervention as a matter of principle and a belief that the individual has inviolable rights. Affirmative action is rejected, the argument runs, because it entails government intervention and because it sacrifices the right of the individual not to be discriminated against or, alternatively, because it requires the sacrifice of an individual's right to a "group right," which on this view is not really a right at all since the only real rights are individual rights. So viewed, white Americans oppose affirmative action because they are committed to the American value of individualism. A third question, then, is:

> To what extent does opposition to affirmative action reflect a distinctively American resistance to the use of government authority to rectify societal problems?

It is additionally argued that white opposition to affirmative action is a function of the fact that whites, merely by virtue of being whites, cannot benefit from it. So viewed, the reason for opposition is neither racial prejudice nor values. It is group interest.[4] A fourth question, then, is this:

> To what extent does opposition to affirmative action reflect an aversion to the use of affirmative action to help blacks distinctively?

A fifth, and more radical, question is also worth asking. Public opinion studies of race rest on a precarious assumption: that white Americans, when asked how they feel about affirmative action for black Americans, will answer honestly.[5] But surely some whites wish to avoid expressing their true view on affirmative action because it is controversial and they do not care for controversy; or because they fear that if they object to affirmative action they will appear racist; or even because they dislike how their complaints about affirmative action sound to their own ears. And owing to this self-censorship, whatever its particular motive, the impression we have of the politics of affirmative action may be very misleading. Thus, the last question we will ask in this chapter is:

> If citizens have a chance to express their feelings about affirmative action in absolute privacy, convinced that no one can tell what they really think, what does the politics of affirmative action actually look like?

By way of answers we shall try to demonstrate the following: (1) The role of racial prejudice in promoting opposition to affirmative action is minor. (2) Rather than opposition to affirmative action signaling a refusal to acknowledge the discrimination and exploitation that black Americans have suffered, a substantial majority of white Americans believe that an extra effort should be made to see that blacks are treated fairly. (3) Opposition to affirmative action is not peculiar to Americans. (4) Opposition to affirmative action does not hinge on the race of the group who benefits but rather on whether the procedures involved are judged to be fair. (5) In addition to dislike of blacks leading to dislike of affirmative action, dislike of affirmative action fosters dislike of blacks. (6) Opposition to and resentment over affirmative action has burst conventional political channels—it is now as prevalent on the left, among liberals and Democrats, as on the right, among conservatives and Republicans.

∎ ∎ ∎

In considering the relation between racial prejudice and opposition to affirmative action, a pair of preliminary observations are obvious.[6] On the one hand, racial prejudice surely promotes opposition to affirmative action; on the other, racial prejudice is unlikely to be the only factor promoting opposition. But of course this leaves unanswered the crucial question: Given that prejudice and opposition to affirmative action are related, how large is the relationship between them? Is racial prejudice a major factor in white Americans' rejection of affirmative action, or only a minor one?

The National Election Studies (NES)—a biennial, national public opinion survey conducted by the Center for Political Studies at the University of Michigan, and the most widely used public opinion survey in political science—has monitored the opinions of Americans about affirmative action in two domains—in hiring and promotions, and in college and university admissions. With respect to jobs, the issue was posed this way:

> Some people say that because of past discrimination blacks should be given preference in hiring and promotion. Others say that such preference in hiring and promotion of blacks is wrong because it gives blacks advantages they have not earned. What about your opinion—are you for or against preferential hiring and promotion of blacks?

With respect to education, the question ran:

> Some people say that because of past discrimination it is sometimes necessary for colleges and universities to reserve openings for blacks students. Others oppose quotas because they say quotas give blacks advantages they have not earned. What about your opinion—are you for or against quotas to admit black students?

Strong, not weak, forms of affirmative action are under consideration here—preferential treatment with respect to jobs, quotas with respect to college admission. But opinions are being solicited with a sensitivity to the role of race as an issue in American history. People are not just being asked their position on affirmative action in and of itself, without regard to historical context. Rather they are explicitly reminded of one of the principal arguments in behalf of affirmative action—namely, that blacks have historically been discriminated against.

From this survey we have, then, measures of Americans' attitudes toward affirmative action in two contexts—hiring and college admissions. In addition, in 1992 the National Election Studies included a direct measure of racial prejudice. Every respondent was asked to evaluate "whites in general" in three respects—the extent to which they were hardworking versus lazy, intelligent versus unintelligent, and peaceful versus violent.[7] They then were asked to evaluate "blacks in general" in the same three respects. For everyone, then, we can tell whether, and to what extent, they believe blacks are less intelligent, lazier, and more violent than whites. The more nega-

tive evaluations of blacks that a white makes, the more prejudiced he or she is; the fewer negative evaluations, the less
prejudiced he or she is.[8]

To what extent does racial prejudice drive whites to oppose
affirmative action? Consider whites at the 75th percentile in
terms of racial prejudice—that is, who are more prejudiced
than 3 out of every 4 whites (see figure 1). Nine out of every
ten of *them* oppose affirmative action in hiring.[9]

To observe that whites who cannot abide blacks reject special efforts to assist them fits common sense exactly. But what
is not at all a matter of common sense is the response of whites
who do *not* dislike blacks. Among those whites whose attitudes
toward blacks are neither especially positive nor especially
negative, more than 8 out of 10 objected to affirmative action
in jobs; in education, just over 7 out of 10 objected to affirmative action. By any standard, to find so completely one-sided
opposition on the part of people in the middle is striking.

However, to see how fallacious it is to attribute opposition
to affirmative action mainly to racial prejudice, look at the
probability of opposition on the part of whites who are the
most positive in their attitudes toward blacks. Consider, to
make the point unequivocally, the most racially tolerant 1
percent of whites. Approximately 8 out of every 10 of them
oppose affirmative action in hiring, and about 6 out of every
10 oppose it in college admissions. In short, even if we set aside
99 out of 100 whites, and look only at the 1 percent of whites
who feel the most respect and sympathy for blacks, opposition
to affirmative action is one-sided.

Considering the charge that opposition to affirmative action
is driven by racial intolerance, it is striking that race-conscious
policies are overwhelmingly rejected even by the uncommonly
racially tolerant. We would emphasize that both in the case of
preferential treatment in hiring and of racial quotas in educational admissions, the influence of racial prejudice is statistically significant, answering to the common sense intuition

FIGURE 1
White Opposition to Affirmative Action, by Level of Prejudice

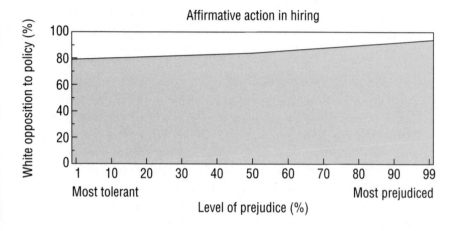

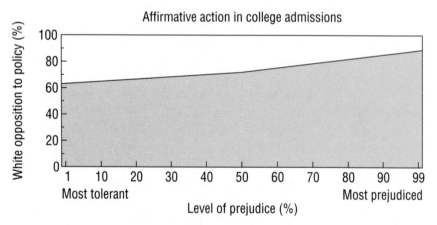

Source: 1992 National Election Study. The number of respondents ranges from 1,673 to 1,708. The level of prejudice corresponds to specific points on the distribution of prejudice, when the respondents are arranged from most tolerant to most prejudiced. Tests for statistical significance, impact of prejudice: opposition to affirmative action in hiring, $t = 3.94$, $p < 0.001$; opposition to affirmative action in college admission, $t = 5.47$, $p < 0.001$.

that whites who cannot abide blacks are even more likely to object to affirmative action than are whites who feel sympathy and positive regard for them. But the fundamental fact is that race prejudice, far from dominating and orchestrating the opposition to affirmative action, makes only a slight contribution to it.[10]

■　■　■

Those most sympathetic to the need for overcoming the historic injustices of race see in the intensity of opposition to affirmative action evidence of the intransigence of white America. Adding fresh insult to past injury, affirmative action, which is intended to secure a level playing field for blacks and other minorities, is now criticized on the ground that it works against equal opportunity. Hence the irony: the call has gone up for a color-blind society, as part of an effort to undercut the policy most instrumental in achieving racial equality— namely, affirmative action. Is opposition to affirmative action, now justified as a defense of equal opportunity, in fact driven by a refusal to recognize that African Americans deserve special consideration?

In order to get some leverage on these issues, consider the history and meaning of affirmative action. The term itself first appeared in a presidential order issued by President Kennedy in March 1961. Revising previous executive orders, he supplemented the negative injunction not to discriminate with the positive duty to see that discrimination does not occur.[11] In the words of the order, "The contractor will take affirmative action to ensure that applicants are employed, and that employees are treated during employment, without regard to their race, creed, color, or national origin."[12]

On this initial view of affirmative action, blacks could not be put at a disadvantage in getting a job or winning a promotion because they were black. But neither could whites be put at a disadvantage because they were white. "Preferential treatment" or "racial balancing" to achieve a balance between the proportion of blacks employed by a business and the proportion of blacks living in the community or participating in the available work force was specifically forbidden in the 1964 Civil Rights Act itself.[13]

The passage of the 1964 Civil Rights law was almost immediately followed by the Watts riot, which initiated nearly a half decade of large-scale, big-city race riots. Partly by way of response, the federal government changed the meaning of affirmative action. It required proportional hiring under "goals and timetables," and, through the Equal Employment Opportunity Commission, it redefined the concept of discrimination, arguing (as the Supreme Court later held) that "good intent or absence of discriminatory intent" was irrelevant and that a proof of "disparate impact" sufficed. Between the two actions, affirmative action was reborn, encompassing from this point forward preferential treatment and racial quotas.

Affirmative action, then, may have two meanings. It may mean making positive efforts to ensure that applicants are considered fairly and not excluded or handicapped in competing to get a job or promotion, to win a government contract, or to obtain admission to a school because of their race, creed, color, gender, or national origin. It also may mean ensuring, through preferential treatment, that African Americans receive special preference or advantage in getting hired, obtaining a government contract, or being admitted to school. We have, therefore, devised an experiment in the Race and Politics Study to assess the popular appeal of these two different meanings of affirmative action.

In the Two Meanings Experiment, 1 out of every 2 respondents, randomly selected, was asked:

> Some people say that because of past discrimination, qualified blacks should be given preference in university admissions. Others say that this is wrong because it discriminates against whites. How do you feel—are you in favor or opposed to giving qualified blacks preference in admission to colleges and universities?

By contrast, the other half of respondents were asked:

> Some people say that because of past discrimination, an extra effort should be made to make sure that qualified blacks are considered for university admission. Others say that this extra effort is wrong because it discriminates against whites. How do you feel—are you in favor or opposed to making an extra effort to make sure qualified blacks are considered for admission to colleges and universities?

Whether a person is asked about affirmative action in the sense of preferential treatment or of making an extra effort is decided on an entirely random basis. This assures that the half of the sample asked about the one is identical to the half asked about the other in every respect (for example, education, political outlook, or even degree of racial prejudice), chance differences aside. This randomization guarantees that any difference in reactions to the two versions of affirmative action are a function of the difference between the policies, not a function of any differences among the people asked about them.

But why ask only some people their view of affirmative action defined in terms of preferential treatment and others their view of affirmative action defined as making an extra effort? Why not ask everyone his or her view of both? The answer: precisely because the issue of affirmative action is so controversial. Suppose we first asked people's views of affirmative action in the sense of preferential treatment for blacks, then their opinion about making an extra effort to assure fair consideration for qualified blacks. If more support is shown for "making an extra effort" than for "preferential treatment," it would always be reasonable to be suspicious about that result. After all, by asking first about preferential treatment and then about extra effort, we have presented people with a ready-made opportunity to show, in their second answer, that the opposition to affirmative action expressed in their first answer should not be taken to mean that they are opposed across-the-board to helping blacks.

We do, however, want to underline that both conceptions involve affirmative action. Both call for blacks to get *special attention*. Thus, to support the initial "extra effort" version of affirmative action requires more than a readiness to say that everyone, black and white, should be treated alike; it demands, additionally and explicitly, a willingness to make an extra effort in order to assure that African Americans specifically are being treated fairly. In the case of both, moreover, there is an explicit reminder that to engage in either form of affirmative action may be "wrong because it discriminates against whites." Thus supplied with a socially legitimate reason to oppose affirmative action in either form, it will be the more impressive if whites nonetheless support it, at least in its original sense of making an extra effort to ensure fair consideration of blacks.

What difference does the definition of affirmative action make? Consider first preferential treatment in regard to college admissions (figure 2). Even though blacks who would be admitted to university are explicitly described as "qualified," only about a quarter of whites support preferential treatment for them. What is more, of the 75 percent who oppose preferential treatment, more than half (almost 40 percent of all whites) object to it strongly. An overwhelming and intense majority is thus arrayed against affirmative action which involves special treatment. Consider, by contrast, making an extra effort to assure fair consideration for blacks in college admissions. Now, nearly two thirds of all whites surveyed support rather than oppose this form of affirmative action, and more than a fourth are strongly in favor of it.

The Two Meanings Experiment thus suggests a lesson about the moral climate of opinion now surrounding the issue of race in America. Partly out of sincere conviction, partly from tactical considerations, public commentary on race tends to represent the climate of opinion prevailing in white America as sour—indifferent to the special burdens blacks have borne, unsympathetic to appeals for fairness in their behalf. Opposition to affirmative action is taken to indicate white intransi-

FIGURE 2
Two Meanings Experiment

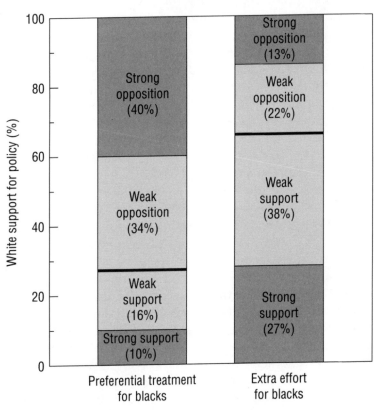

Source: 1991 Race and Politics Study. Number of Respondents: 887 and 911. Tests for statistical significance: extra effort vs. preferential treatment, $t = 16.59$, $p < 0.001$.

gence, proof of either their indifference or outright opposition to achieving fairness for blacks. There is, unmistakably, bitterness and resentment over affirmative action. But it is a mistake to draw from the observation that many whites are angry over affirmative action the conclusion that they have turned their backs on black Americans. The actual climate of opinion in white America runs, if anything, in the contrary direction. The balance of sympathy, rather than opposing, runs in favor of making an extra effort to assure fairness for blacks. As the Two Meanings Experiment demonstrates, a clear majority supports not merely the importance of giving blacks fair consideration in the abstract but going the extra mile in practice to ensure they really are fairly treated.

Beyond this, the results of the Two Meanings Experiment help pinpoint the aspect of affirmative action that evokes so extensive and intense opposition. Consider how the issue is framed in the experiment. In the "extra effort" condition, just as in the "preferential treatment" one, the idea is that blacks applying to college will receive special attention: indeed, the whole point is that special attention is necessary to ensure that qualified blacks are not overlooked or given short shrift for any reason. The point, though, is that special attention is necessary and appropriate to make sure that they are judged by the same standards as everybody else. It is wrong for them to be judged by standards that are tougher just because they are black. But for the very same reason it is wrong for whites to be judged by tougher standards just because they are white. So a clear majority of whites believe that affirmative action should be undertaken to assure that decisions affecting blacks have been made fairly. And an even larger majority object to affirmative action when it means that blacks will receive not special attention but special treatment.

Much of the politics of affirmative action centers on arguments about its unpopularity. Setting to one side the longstanding contention that opposition to affirmative action is fueled chiefly by race prejudice, which the objective evidence has shown to be wrong, let us examine the now commonly advanced contention that opposition to affirmative action has flared up because prospects for the future have become clouded over. According to this argument, whites, and more particularly white men, are being squeezed economically in the 1990s. It is harder for them to get a job, or keep it, or get ahead in it. The real problem in fact is not affirmative action, the argument runs. It is instead structural changes in the economy, above all, the twin pincer movement of deindustrialization, which has resulted in the loss of blue-collar jobs, and of corporate downsizing, which has resulted in the loss of white-collar jobs. And as these deeper-lying changes in the economy have worked their way through, whites—above all, young white males—have seen their prospects for a successful career and a good life shrink. In their concern and incomprehension over their fading future, they have taken out their frustration and anger on an immediately visible target—namely, affirmative action.

If this line of argument is correct, then at least three things should be true. First, opposition to affirmative action should wax in economically hard times, and wane in economically good times. Second, opposition to affirmative action should be more pronounced for those who, because they are at the start of their careers, are more vulnerable to government hiring and promoting pressures, and less marked for those who, because they are near the end of theirs, are less vulnerable to government intervention. Finally, opposition should be more pronounced among white men, and particularly young white men, than among white women, whether young or old, since white women in fact benefit, rather than suffer, from affirmative action programs.

In the two top charts in figure 3 we plot opposition to affirmative action among all whites, at two-year intervals between 1986 (the first year it was measured) and 1994 (the most recent), using the NES biennial surveys. Over this period, all the political rhetoric to the contrary notwithstanding, white attitudes have not changed a whit. A decade ago, at the height of the prosperity of the 1980s, more than 80 percent of whites opposed preferential treatment in hiring. Almost as many

FIGURE 3
White Opposition to Affirmative Action, by Age and Sex

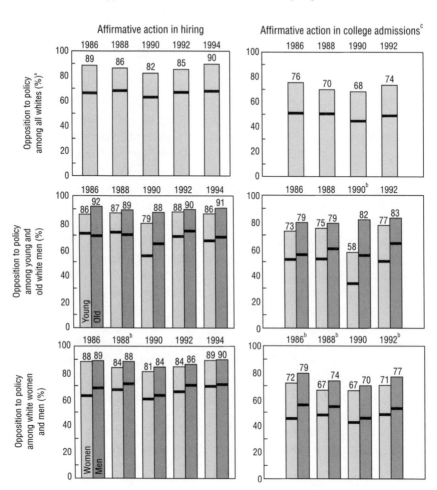

Source: 1986 to 1994 National Election Study. The portion of each bar above the solid line represents strong opposition to the policy. Number of respondents: Affirmative action in college admissions, all whites, from 800 to 1,842; young white men, from 88 to 204; old white men, from 76 to 176; white men, from 364 to 882; white women, from 463 to 960. Affirmative action in hiring, all whites, from 809 to 1880; young white men, from 91 to 213; old white men, from 80 to 185; white men, from 368 to 907; white women, from 441 to 973.

a. Statistical test for a trend over time: affirmative action in hiring, $t = 1.20$, $p < 0.230$; affirmative action in college admissions, $t = 0.66$, $p < 0.505$.

b. Statistically significant at the .05 level.

c. This question was not asked in the 1994 National Election Study.

whites, roughly 75 percent, opposed reserving places for black college students. Since then, the overall numbers have not budged an inch, nor has the intensity of opposition softened in any degree. It sounds reasonable to say that whites now oppose affirmative action because in the more economically competitive 90s they have become more concerned about their own economic prospects. But that statement is wrong. Just as many opposed affirmative action, and just as intensely, from the first day it became identified with preferential treatment.

White men who are younger and only starting their careers are at higher risk of being negatively affected by affirmative action than are those who are older and have the largest part of their working careers behind them. But as the two middle charts in figure 3 show, rather than younger white males being more opposed to affirmative action than older ones, so far as they differ, the difference is just the other way around. It is the older, not the younger, who are the more likely to be opposed.

Finally, the bottom pair of charts show the positions of women and men on affirmative action. By close inspection, it is possible to identify occasional points of difference, but without exception, they are small and politically insignificant. The simple reality is that the overwhelming number of women, just like the overwhelming number of men, oppose affirmative action. The gender gap over preferential treatment is as specious as the age gap.

The central lesson of this National Election Studies series is the untenability of all the current interpretations which attempt to particularize opposition to affirmative action, claiming it to be concentrated in one or another comparatively narrow part of the public at large. On the contrary, as these data demonstrate, opposition to affirmative action was and is intense, unvarying, and above all pervasive.

■　■　■

Public commentators on affirmative action, altogether appropriately, often have a position on it themselves. If they support it, it is naturally difficult for them to grasp, to sympathize with, or even to recognize the reasons why others oppose it. They understand the background from which affirmative action emerged. They are keenly aware that blacks do not yet enjoy a level playing field. They know the purpose of affirmative action is to put things right. It is, in consequence, tempting for them to believe that their fellow citizens would support it too but for the fact that it aims to benefit blacks or, alternatively, but for the fact that, as Americans, they tend to be committed to individualism and hence opposed to strong government action to assure equality of opportunity.

By way of testing both ideas simultaneously—that is, racial prejudice and American individualism—our colleagues in Great Britain carried out a special experiment in our behalf to assess public attitudes toward affirmative action mandating group quotas in employment.[14] The political culture there, as compared to here, is manifestly more favorable to collectivist policies, less in the thrall of an ethic of individual responsibility, achievement, and self-reliance.

In the British Quota Experiment, the group to benefit from affirmative action was experimentally manipulated. Our reason for the manipulation was two-fold. The first was to establish to what extent opposition to affirmative action which mandates quotas is opportunistically a function of a reluctance to benefit minorities distinctively. Do whites oppose for blacks what they would favor for fellow whites? To see whether this was so, one third of the time the group to benefit was women, and one third of the time it was blacks and Asians. But since we wanted to explore further the nature of the objection to preferential treatment, we also chose a group that might attract substantial support. Proceeding on the assumption that it is more imperative to help those who, for reasons beyond their control, find it harder to help themselves, we chose as the final group to benefit from affirmative action the disabled.[15]

Our results show that opinion about affirmative action to

FIGURE 4
British Quota Experiment

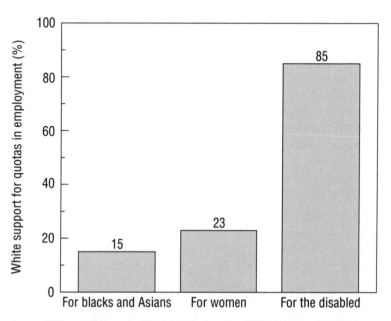

Source: William L. Miller, ed., *Alternatives to Freedom* (1995). Number of respondents: 2,060. The differences between the percentages for all comparisons are significant at least at the .01 level.

benefit minorities is as one-sided in England as in America (see figure 4). Approximately 85 percent of whites surveyed in England opposed quotas for blacks and Asians in hiring. Quotas were also overwhelmingly opposed when the beneficiaries of preferential treatment were women: more than 75 percent of whites surveyed opposed quotas. There was, however, an intriguing exception to British opposition to affirmative action. Among whites, 85 percent favored affirmative action, in the strong sense of imposing quotas, when the beneficiaries were the disabled. It obviously *can* make a difference who is to be helped: affirmative action, in this experiment, was one-sidedly endorsed for the disabled, and just as one-sidedly rejected for minorities and women.

Acknowledging this, we draw two conclusions from the British Quota Experiment. First, since opposition to quotas is as common there as here, it cannot be that opposition to affirmative action in the United States is rooted in distinctively American values, whether individualism or any other. Second, since opposition to quotas is as common when women are to benefit as when minorities will, the basis of opposition to affirmative action cannot be race itself.[16] To most people, unless those who are to be helped manifestly cannot help themselves, it seems wrong to award a job on the basis of group membership rather than on the basis of individual merit. The British results thus demonstrate that little is specifically racial, and still less is distinctively American, about the rejection of affirmative action.

■　■　■

Support in Great Britain for affirmative action for the disabled calls attention to the way in which judgments about affirmative action can be tied to people's ideas about fairness. In this case, they center on the shared intuition that those who, for reasons beyond their control, are handicapped in helping themselves are entitled to help from others. To see how considerations of fairness can promote as well as undercut support for affirmative action, we also looked where support would seem least, not most, likely—the imposition of explicit racial quotas in private industry in America.

A primary basis for the one-sided opposition to affirmative action which involves preferential treatment or explicit quotas is the belief that it is not fair to hire people for jobs or grant them admission to schools because they belong to a particular social group and not because they are the most qualified. On the other hand, the deepest argument *for* preferential treatment for blacks is that they still can be treated so unfairly. What we want to do, therefore, is to see whether white Americans, their normal aversion to racial quotas notwithstanding, will see discrimination in favor of blacks in a different light if it assists blacks who actually have been victims of discrimination.

The Justification Experiment accordingly describes three conditions. In the baseline condition, one third of the sample, randomly selected, was asked the following question:

> Do you think that large companies should be required to give a certain number of jobs to blacks, or should the government stay out of this?

In the other two conditions, respondents were presented with a justification of racial quotas, but the specific justification varied. Thus, in one condition, they were told, "There are some large companies with employment policies that discriminate against blacks," and then asked if these companies should be required to give a certain number of jobs to blacks. By contrast, the final third of the respondents were told, "There are some large companies where blacks are underrepresented," and then asked whether a certain number of jobs should be given to blacks.

It does not necessarily follow that, if a company has been found to discriminate against blacks, actual quotas are right. A person can feel genuinely outraged at racial discrimination, yet still believe that racial quotas are morally inappropriate. But if a central part of opposition to affirmative action is grounded in considerations of fairness, as we have suggested, then it should matter to many whites if a company has a history of directly discriminating against blacks. And if it does matter, they may be willing, if a company has discriminated against blacks, to support what they would otherwise believe to be unfair.

This is exactly what we found to be the case (see figure 5).

FIGURE 5
Justification Experiment

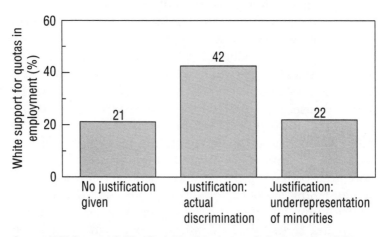

Source: 1991 Race and Politics Study. Number of respondents ranges from 665 to 749. Tests of statistical significance for the effect of the different conditions: no justification vs. actual discrimination, $t = 6.42$, $p < 0.001$; no justification vs. underrepresentation, $t = 0.73$, $p < 0.466$; actual discrimination vs. underrepresentation, $t = 7.35$, $p < 0.001$.

When no specific argument was made in behalf of affirmative action, approximately 20 percent of whites supported it. By contrast, when whites were told that the company had discriminated against blacks in the past, approximately 40 percent of whites supported racial quotas. This is not an absolute majority, but it is not very far off, and it is foolish to suppose that policies come into play in policies only if they command the support of 50 percent plus one.

It is thus possible to build substantial support for affirmative action as a response to actual discrimination, even when it explicitly involves racial quotas. Does this mean that opposition to race-conscious policies can possibly be turned around by public argument and education? If time and care are taken to explain that quotas are being imposed to put right past discrimination, can a sizeable number of white citizens—possibly not an absolute majority, but politically a significant portion of the informed public—be brought around in support of affirmative action in the strong sense?

In liberal circles of opinion, the argument is frequently made that popular opposition to affirmative action represents either a lack of information or misinformation about its real purposes. Citizens, according to this view, would feel differently about affirmative action programs if they knew what these programs actually are attempting to achieve and why they were put into effect in the first place. Hence the need, apart from correcting the occasional and atypical abuse, for programs of public education. If the public knew that affirmative action was a response to the way blacks are discriminated against and treated unfairly, citizens would agree that it was fair. And isn't this what the Justification Experiment shows?

The heart of the matter is the term "discrimination." It is widely acknowledged, even by those most sympathetic to affirmative action programs, that racial discrimination, in the sense of intentionally treating blacks worse because they are black, is difficult as a rule to demonstrate and in any event is no longer widespread among the institutions most faithfully committed to carrying out affirmative action—such as colleges and universities. And precisely because intentional discrimination is difficult to demonstrate, those who are sympathetic to achieving racial equality have argued that the notion of discrimination, which in its standard meaning refers to situations in which a person or company treats blacks unfairly because they are black, has to be differently defined. According to the new definition, discrimination refers instead to situations in which blacks do not do as well as whites—say, are not hired at the same rate—and this observed difference, or disparate impact, in and of itself is presumptive evidence of discrimination.[17]

The Justification Experiment also assesses responses to affirmative action where discrimination is defined as disparate impact. In the third condition of the experiment, the justification for affirmative action is explicitly that "there are some large companies where blacks are underrepresented." But this justification has no persuasive power among whites. They were no more likely, if the justification of affirmative action was described in terms of disparate impact, to support it than they were when presented with no justification whatever; that is, almost 80 percent opposed racial quotas despite the disparate impact of a company's hiring policies.

It is a temptation, particularly to those who most wish to assist blacks, to believe that the idea of discrimination can and should be defined in the way most useful to achieving racial equality. It is a temptation because, in both courts and administrative agencies, the redefinition of discrimination from intentional harm to disparate impact has been strikingly successful. But this requires silently substituting a conception of discrimination which ordinary citizens do not share, in order to trade on their moral repugnance at discrimination as it is commonly understood, for the purpose of justifying a program which under normal circumstances seems to them to be itself discriminatory.

■ ■ ■

Some people get worked up when they talk about affirmative action. When whites describe why they think racial quotas are unjust, it is almost possible to hear their teeth grinding. Certainly, the anger and resentment many whites feel about racial preferences has been palpable in our interviews. Reflecting on this, we came to wonder about the consequences. Was it possible that, because whites believe the policy to be unfair and dislike it so intensely, they wind up disliking those who benefit from it? If so, then instead of promoting a society in which race matters less, race-conscious programs will encourage one in which race is more invidious than ever.

To answer this question we conducted the Mere Mention

Experiment.[18] In this study, one half of the respondents were asked their opinion about affirmative action; specifically, the question put to them was:

> In a nearby state, an effort is being made to increase dramatically the number of blacks working in state government. This means that a large number of jobs will be reserved for blacks, even if their scores on merit exams are lower than those of whites who are turned down for the job. Do you favor or oppose the policy?

Then, having given their view of affirmative action, they were asked to describe what most blacks are like. The other half of respondents were asked exactly the same questions but in precisely the reverse order. First they were asked what most blacks are like; then they were asked their view of affirmative action.

In the Mere Mention Experiment, affirmative action refers not to making an extra effort to assure fair consideration but to mandating racial quotas and preferential treatment. Moreover, when the issue of affirmative action was presented, the inevitable consequence of imposing it—that blacks with lower scores on merit tests will get jobs while whites with higher scores are turned down—was specifically noted. On the other side, the question deliberately asked about affirmative action not in the respondent's own state but rather in a "nearby state," in order to minimize the likelihood that people will respond angrily to affirmative action because they feel that they themselves or members of their family will be directly hurt by it.

The power of the Mere Mention Experiment follows from the randomization of the sequence of the two questions. This randomization means that members of the two halves of the sample are alike in education, social background, basic prejudice, political outlook, present circumstances; indeed, purely chance differences aside, alike in every respect but one. The only way the two halves differ is that one half is asked first about affirmative action and then about blacks, and the other half is asked first about blacks and then about affirmative action. It follows that, if the reactions of the two halves toward blacks differ, then the only factor that could possibly have caused this difference is the mere mention of affirmative action.

Whites who have just been asked to give an opinion about affirmative action are significantly more likely to describe "most blacks" as "lazy" than are whites to whom affirmative action has not been mentioned (see figure 6). In addition, they are significantly more likely to describe them as "irresponsible" and "arrogant," although this last difference does not quite reach standard levels of statistical significance. In short, merely bringing up the subject of affirmative action significantly increases dislike of blacks.

Affirmative action is not the primary reason why whites

FIGURE 6
Mere Mention Experiment

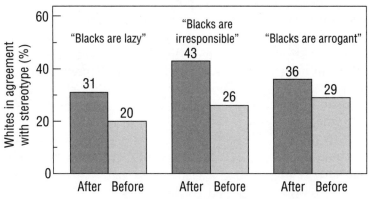

... the mere mention of affirmative action

Source: 1989 Lexington, Kentucky, Survey. Number of respondents: total 236, minimum base 114. Tests of statistical significance: after versus before: lazy, $p < 0.05$; irresponsible, $p < 0.05$; arrogant, $p < 0.10$.

dislike blacks. Large numbers of them disliked blacks before racial quotas were ever dreamed of; large numbers would have continued to dislike blacks if affirmative action had never been conceived of; and large numbers will dislike blacks in the future even if affirmative action comes to an immediate and total end. Still, the Mere Mention Experiment illustrates the power of affirmative action to engender ill will. The impact of the experiment is, in quantitative terms, not large. What is impressive is that merely changing the order of the questions should have made any difference whatsoever. After all, no effort was made to whip up feelings about affirmative action. No one was exposed to the equivalent of a "Willie Horton" advertisement. They did not even take part in an extended discussion of affirmative action, allowing them to get worked up. The Mere Mention Experiment consists only in varying the order of one question in an interview made up of a hundred or more questions. Nonetheless, the mere mention of affirmative action turns out to sharpen hostility to blacks.

▪ ▪ ▪

The standard story of the politics of affirmative action is straightforward. Under Franklin Roosevelt, Harry Truman, and John Kennedy, liberalism and the Democratic party became, broadly, the political voice of the disadvantaged; then under Johnson, both undertook to act in behalf of the racially oppressed specifically—a political transformation climaxing in the historic passage in 1964 of the Civil Rights Act and in 1965 of the Voting Rights Act.

In the standard story, then, the battle over affirmative action is an episode in a larger war which over the last half century has seen liberals and the Democratic party predominantly lining up on one side and conservatives and the Republican party on the other.[19] And, consistent with this story, liberals and conservatives differ on the new race-conscious agenda itself. People who label themselves conservatives are twice as likely as those who call themselves liberals to object to making an extra effort to ensure that qualified blacks are considered for college admission (see figure 7). Conservatives are also significantly more likely than liberals to oppose preferences for qualified blacks in admission to colleges. For that matter, conservatives are also significantly more likely than liberals to oppose requiring large companies to give a number of jobs to blacks. And finally, conservatives are significantly more likely than liberals to be angry about blacks and other minorities getting special advantages in jobs and schools. In short, just as supposed, there is an ideological division over the new race-conscious agenda (see figure 7).

But common sense suggests that people do not always say what they really think about issues of race. Sometimes they choose to say nothing; sometimes to say, not what they think, but what they think they are supposed to say. But how, then, can we tell what they really do think?

By means of a technique called the List Experiment, we have found a way to tell how Americans feel about affirmative action without their knowing that we can tell how they feel.[20] In the baseline condition, which contains one half of a random sample of interviewees, the interviewer begins by saying,

> I'm going to read you a list of three things that sometimes make people angry or upset. After I read all three, just tell me HOW MANY of them upset you. I don't want to know which ones, just how many.

Then, the interviewer reads a list of three items:

> the federal government increasing the tax on gasoline; professional athletes getting million-dollar-plus salaries; large corporations polluting the environment.

In the test condition, the interviewer begins again by saying that she is going to read a list of some things that sometimes make people angry or upset. Again she instructs the respon-

FIGURE 7
White Opposition to Affirmative Action, by Ideology

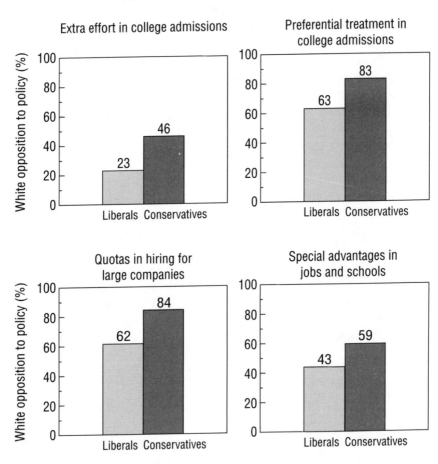

Source: 1991 Race and Politics Study. Number of respondents ranges from 78 to 313. Tests of statistical significance, comparing liberals to conservatives: extra effort in college admissions, $t = 4.28$, $p < 0.001$ preferential treatment in college admissions, $t = 3.90$, $p < 0.001$; quotas in hiring for large companies, $t = 3.60$, $p < 0.001$; special advantages in jobs and schools, $t = 4.11$, $p < 0.001$.

dent that all she wants to know is *HOW MANY* of them upset him. Again she warns him, "I don't want to know which ones, just how many." But this time she reads a list of *four* items. The first three are exactly the same. The last item is:

black leaders asking the government for affirmative action.

Suppose our hypothetical respondent in the test condition is offended by the princely sums that professional athletes now earn and also is upset by affirmative action. Asked how many items on the list make him angry, he answers, "two." In answering "two," he knows that there is no way for the interviewer to tell that one of the two things that makes him angry is affirmative action.

And he is absolutely right.[21] But the analyst can calculate in a microsecond the proportion of people in the sample as a whole who are angry over affirmative action. Suppose one point is given for every item that makes people angry. Suppose also that the average number of items that make people angry in the baseline condition is 1.0; and that the average number of items that make people angry in the affirmative action condition is 1.5. Since three of the items are exactly the same in the two experimental conditions, and since the two subsamples being interviewed are identical except for chance, we can assume that had the item on affirmative action not been included, the mean in the second condition would also have been 1.0. It follows that, to generate an increment of 0.5, one half of the respondents in the test condition must have gotten angry over affirmative action. Thus, even when it is not possible to tell which individuals are upset, it is possible to tell how many upset individuals there are.

Through the List Experiment, then, we can tell how people feel about affirmative action, without their knowing we can tell how they feel. And this allows us to establish how liberals *really* feel about affirmative action. As we have seen, when they are asked directly, liberals are markedly less likely than conservatives to say they are angry over it. But this appearance of an ideological cleavage over the new race-conscious agenda is, we suspect, largely an illusion, a result of liberals saying what they think they should say, not what they really think.

By way of determining whether our suspicion is true or not, we compare liberals and conservatives' likelihood of anger about affirmative action as revealed by the List Experiment.[22] It turns out that about 57 percent of white liberals include "black leaders asking the government for affirmative action" among the things that make them angry or upset, compared with 50 percent of conservatives (and 55 percent of moderates; see table 1). These three figures are statistically indistinguishable.

Parallel analyses show that the same is true for Democrats and Republicans. When they believe that nobody can tell how they feel, Democrats are just as likely as Republicans to be upset over affirmative action. Specifically, about 65 percent of Democrats and 64 percent of Republicans indicate that they are angry or upset about "black leaders asking the government for affirmative action." Independents are significantly less upset: 40 percent included that item in the list of things that make them angry (see table 1).

In sum, when people feel free to express how they really feel rather than having to say what they think they should say, the politics of affirmative action becomes clear for the first time. Rather than facing the opposition of the right but enjoying the backing of the left—which is the standard pattern for redistributive politics—affirmative action runs into trouble on both sides of the political aisle. It is as resented on the left as on the right.

Just as far as this is true, the issue of race now is divisive in a way it was not before. Instead of deepening the cleavage between the political left (liberals and the Democratic party) and the political right (conservatives and the Republican party), resentment over affirmative action has burst through the usual

TABLE 1
Covert White Anger over Affirmative Action, by Ideology and Partisanship (List Experiment)

Respondents, by ideology and partisanship	Number of items that anger respondents		
	When affirmative action is not on the list	When affirmative action is on the list	Difference[a]
Liberals	1.97	2.54	0.57
Moderates	2.04	2.59	0.55
Conservatives	2.18	2.68	0.50
Democrats	2.23	2.88	0.65
Independents	2.17	2.57	0.40
Republicans	2.19	2.83	0.64

Source: 1991 Race and Politics Study. Number of respondents: for ideology, from 92 to 159; for partisanship, from 173 to 201.

a. Difference is significant at .001 level for all items.

ideological channels. The battle over affirmative action threatens not merely to weaken further support for the liberal Democratic coalition at its periphery but to divide it at its core.

The idea that affirmative action may be as unpopular on the left as on the right occurred to us in the course of carrying out extended interviews with an array of citizens. We were struck by the occasional interjection, and still more by the frequent silence, when liberals had a more ample opportunity than came to them ordinarily to express the full range of their hopes and concerns about affirmative action. Many liberals, it seemed to us, were being more than ordinarily careful in what they choose to say. But it seemed that they were being careful not because they cared what *we* thought about what they said but because *they* cared about it themselves. Liberals were refraining from saying what they thought about affirmative action, it seemed to us, not because they feared the disapproval of others but because they did not like how their words about affirmative action sounded to their own ears.

It has, of course, become a reflex for many to express attitudes critical of some aspect or other of contemporary racial politics and then add, in embarrassment and apology, that they hope they do not sound like a racist, because truly they are not. The more closely we listened to expressions like this, the more they seemed to testify not to a wish to cover up opposition to racial equality but to a desire to reaffirm commitment to it. Precisely because they genuinely care about the plight of black Americans, white liberals are especially likely, in public, to muffle their own criticisms of affirmative action.

The reluctance of liberals to express publicly their criticisms and anger over affirmative offers a key to the politics of race. Liberal, Democratic activists offer more unqualified support for affirmative action than is obviously consistent with their electoral well-being. Yet, it does not seem reasonable to suppose that they are distinctively indifferent to their political self-interest. Nor is it reasonable to believe that they are specially inept at reading the public mood. Why, then, have they persisted in championing affirmative action?

Part of the answer, we want to suggest, has to do with misreading sentiment not in the public taken as a whole—even politicians of below-average astuteness have long recognized the unpopularity of preferential treatment and racial quotas in the country as a whole—but that portion of it on their own side of the political aisle. When it comes to public issues, most people spend most of their time speaking to those who mostly agree with them. The inclination of liberal Democrats to avoid public criticism of affirmative action has led liberal Democratic activists to overestimate support for, and to underestimate anger at, affirmative action on their own side of the political aisle. The consequence: an emerging tension between liberalism and the commitment to racial equality.

The results of the List Experiment suggest that the politics of affirmative action is not merely cutting into the liberal Democratic coalition at its periphery but threatening to split it at its core. This result, if valid, manifestly matters not just to political analysts but to politicians and the public at large. So it is important to probe any limitations of the List Experiment. The experiment seems to us open to criticism on three grounds. Most crucially, it is designed to persuade respondents that the interviewer cannot guess which things make them angry just from knowing how many make them angry. But the list is only three items long in the baseline condition, and by chance roughly 4 in 10 respondents objected to all three in the baseline condition. Some respondents in the affirmative action condition, it follows, may have been inhibited from expressing anger at affirmative action, since their only option would have been to say that all four items in the test condition made them angry, thereby exposing the fact that one of the items upsetting them was black leaders asking for government action. It is unlikely, in view of detailed mathematical analyses of the List Experiment results, that this occurred. It is, however, important to lay this potential problem to rest.

A second potential weakness: Consider the wording of the test item in the affirmative action condition, "black leaders asking the government for affirmative action." The item, in terms of strict content, encompasses attitudes toward two distinguishable components—how whites feel about black leaders and how they feel about affirmative action. It is arguable that the high rates of anger in the List Experiment reflect the unpopularity not just of affirmative action but also of black leaders. Alternatively, the phrase "affirmative action" has come to be a catchbasin for resentment. Because whites have come to abhor a phrase which is ambiguous and invites misunderstanding, it does not necessarily follow that they despise the actual practices it entails. Finally, we have seen that liberals are less likely to be angry over affirmative action if they are asked overtly rather than covertly. But the overt and covert measures, though similar, are not the same, and exact comparison of the two requires that their wording be identical.

It is desirable to replicate the List Experiment for all of these reasons, plus one more. The most convincing proof of the validity of the List Experiment would be to do it all over again and find the same results, above all observing that anger over affirmative action is as common on the political left as on the political right. Desirable as it would be to do this, ordinarily it would be out of the question, since it requires that an entire new study be done. But much hinges on whether affirmative action is dividing the liberal Democratic coalition at its center. Accordingly, to determine whether our initial findings are valid and reliable, we undertook to replicate the List Experiment by conducting an independent study, representative of the country as a whole, in 1994.[23]

In the follow-up study, although for purposes of replication one of the test items ("black leaders asking for affirmative action") remained the same, a number of specific changes in the experiment were made. Most critically, the list in the baseline condition was increased to four.[24] Since the average number of angry responses in the baseline condition was less than two, the problem of "ceiling effects" disappeared.[25] In addition, to avoid relying on just the term "affirmative action" or conflating reactions to affirmative action with responses to black leaders, an additional experimental condition was added, using as a test item "awarding college scholarships on the basis of race." Finally, identical overt and covert measures of anger over affirmative action were used in the follow-up study, taking advantage of an elaborate scheme of randomization to ensure that no respondent assigned to a covert test condition (where an affirmative action item was the last item on the list) was asked the same question in an overt form.[26]

What does the replication of the List Experiment demonstrate? In the original experiment, 55 percent of whites were angry or upset over "black leaders asking the government for affirmative action." In the follow-up experiment, 49 percent proved to be angry or upset over "black leaders asking the government for affirmative action." The two figures are statistically indistinguishable. When the phrase "affirmative action" itself was not used, 61 percent of whites indicated they were angry or upset over "awarding college scholarships on the basis of race." Thus, anger over affirmative action was not merely a response to the vagueness of a term, variously understood; the actual practice of it evoked as much—indeed, more—anger (see table 2).

These results strikingly confirm the basic results of the first study, but of course the crucial question is whether when the List Experiment is conducted a second time it again demonstrates that resentment over the new race-conscious agenda has burst conventional political channels. In the original experiment, when whites felt they could express anger over affirmative action without its being observed, liberals were as likely to be upset as conservatives, Democrats as likely as Republicans. We have done these same calculations for the second trial, which uses identically worded items for direct and indirect measurement, assuring exact comparability (see table 3).[27] Looking first at the overt measures, again we see that conservatives (at 51 percent) are markedly more likely to be angry over affirmative action than liberals (33 percent). But then, turning to the unobtrusive measurement of the List Experiment, again we see that liberals were just as likely to be angry over affirmative action as conservatives (56 percent and 59 percent respectively).[28] A large fraction of liberals, it follows, suppressed overt expression of their anger over preferential treatment and racial quotas. To be sure, so did some conservatives, but to nothing like the same extent. Liberals were between 3 and 4 times as likely to suppress overt expression of anger over affirmative action as conservatives.

Similar results were found when we looked again at party

TABLE 2
Overt and Covert White Anger over Affirmative Action (List Experiment)

		Whites angry over black leaders asking the government for affirmative action (%)	Whites angry over awarding college scholarships on the basis of race (%)
A	Overt measure of affirmative action attitudes	34.1	48.7
B	Covert measure of affirmative action attitudes	49.0	61.1
C	Difference (B−A)	14.9[a]	12.4[a]
D	Unacknowledged anger (C/B)	30.4	20.3

Source: 1994 Multiple Investigator Study. Covert measure is the difference between the number of items that make respondents angry when affirmative action is on the list and when it is not (not shown separately). Number of respondents: for "black leaders," 235 and 483 for the overt and covert measures respectively; for "college scholarships," 201 and 529 for the overt and covert measures respectively.
    a. $p < .05$.

affiliation. Asked directly how they feel about affirmative action, Republicans were significantly more likely to express anger than Democrats (48 percent versus 37 percent). Asked in a way that allowed them to believe they could express anger without anyone being aware of it, Democrats were, if anything, more likely to be angry over affirmative action than Republicans (52 percent of Democrats; 43 percent of Republicans).

It has been our argument that race has become divisive in a new way, and specifically that the liberal Democratic coalition, rather than simply losing support at the edges, among those who least identify with it and are least committed to its principles, is now threatened with a loss of support at its center because of resentment over the new race-conscious agenda.

TABLE 3
Overt and Covert White Anger over Affirmative Action, by Ideology and Partisanship (List Experiment)

By ideology		Liberals (%)	Conservatives (%)	Difference (%)
A	Overt measure of affirmative action attitudes	32.7	50.9	18.2[a]
B	Covert measure of affirmative action attitudes	55.8	59.1	3.3
C	Difference (B−A)	23.1[a]	8.2	
D	Unacknowledged anger (C/B)	41.4	13.9	
By partisanship		Democrats (%)	Republicans (%)	Difference (%)
A	Overt measure of affirmative action attitudes	36.6	48.1	11.5[b]
B	Covert measure of affirmative action attitudes	52.0	43.5	−8.5
C	Difference (B−A)	15.4[a]	n.s.	
D	Unacknowledged anger (C/B)	29.6	n.s.	

Source: 1994 Multiple Investigator Study. Covert measure is the difference between the number of items that make respondents angry when affirmative action is on the list and when it is not, combining "black leaders" and "college scholarships" versions of the question. Number of respondents: for liberals, 46 and 70 for the overt and covert measures, respectively; for conservatives, 101 and 176; for Democrats, 187 and 296; and for Republicans, 214 and 312.

a. p<.05.
b. p<.01.

Among the opponents of affirmative action today, it would seem, are many whites who wish blacks well.

This assertion was tested by comparing groups of whites who are distinguished from one another according to their score on a "racial equality index" (see figure 8). This index assesses the importance whites attach to racial equality and harmony. The higher whites' score on the racial equality index, the less likely they are to be angry about affirmative action—provided they are asked about it directly. However, when they

FIGURE 8
Whites' Anger over Affirmative Action,
by Commitment to Racial Equality

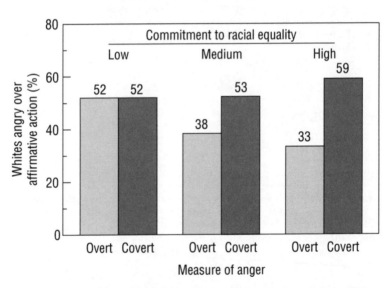

Source: 1994 Multiple Investigator Study. Number of respondents range from 134 to 277. Tests of statistical significance, impact of racial equality: overt measures vs. covert measures for low, n.s.; medium, p < .01; high, p < .01. Low score vs. high score on racial equality index: overt measures, p < .01; covert measures, n.s.

think they can express their feelings unobtrusively, whites who attach the most importance to racial equality are just as likely to be angry or upset over affirmative action as those who attach the least importance to it.

▪ ▪ ▪

Affirmative action, our findings suggest, represents a dilemma for liberalism. On the one hand, it is hard to see how liberalism can maintain a commitment to a program over which it is so deeply divided, and what is more, divided on principle. On the other hand, and just as clearly, it cannot abandon its commitment to affirmative action, partly for reasons of political prudence, partly for reasons of principle. Minorities, together with whites who strongly identify with them, form too large a part of the liberal, Democratic coalition in the public as a whole—and a still larger part of the coalition at the level of activists—to make jettisoning affirmative action feasible. But perhaps equally important, even as many liberals reject affirmative action as a violation of fairness, it has come to symbolize the very commitment to fairness for as many others. The liberal, Democratic coalition, our results suggest, is thus in danger of being politically damned if it continues its commitment to affirmative action, and damned if it does not.

Proponents of affirmative action reject the suggestion that liberalism faces a dilemma. They argue that the liberal, Democratic coalition can continue to sponsor affirmative action and come out ahead. They argue this on two grounds: first, that opposition to affirmative action is very largely "based on misconceptions of how the policy operates";[29] and second, that opposition to affirmative action can be gotten around by redesigning it to be class-based, not race-based.

By way of supporting the first argument, studies are cited showing more public support for affirmative action depending exactly on how it is advanced.[30] If people can be brought to properly understand the experience of blacks in America, the argument runs, common decency will lead them to support affirmative action.

Without being unsympathetic to the emotional arguments being made in the background, we are obliged to say that the evidence is not consistent with such sanguine expectations. As the Two Meanings Experiment demonstrated, although there is substantial support for affirmative action in the sense of making an extra effort to assure fair consideration for blacks and minorities, there is overwhelming opposition to it in the sense of proving preferential treatment. The desire to see blacks fairly treated matters, but it in no way follows that the furor over affirmative action represents, as it were, a terrible misunderstanding. The response to the two policies is different because the two policies are different. To suppose that presenting affirmative action under one description will mollify opposition to it under another misses the point. This is not an argument about words; it is an argument about reality, about what is done and, indeed, what must be done to achieve particular goals.

There are good arguments for affirmative action understood as preferential treatment. If blacks had not been aggressively admitted to undergraduate colleges, medical schools, law schools, and civil service jobs, in part by putting in place a different set of admission standards for blacks, there would not have been a significant number of black doctors, lawyers, engineers, and the like for a generation after the civil rights laws of the 1960s—nor, in all probability, a historic increase in the size of the black middle class. Surely, it is obvious that fair opportunity in American society has been increased precisely through preferential treatment: by increasing access to professions once closed to blacks; by demonstrating blacks' capacity for work and achievement and thus combating racial stereotypes of them as inferior and incapable of success; by providing role models for black children, showing them at first hand what they can achieve; by providing models for *all* children, by introducing them to the true diversity and richness of the American experience.[31] The question now at hand, however, is not whether affirmative action in the sense of preferential treatment was a good idea in the first place. It is instead whether it is a good idea for it to be continued indefinitely.

In coming to grips with *this* question, what we want to underline are the ways that affirmative action now represents a dilemma for liberalism. On the one side, even if it should be conceded that racial prejudice and discrimination are much lower than they were, it can and will be argued that they remain much higher than they should be; and that, even setting aside specifically racial discrimination, the playing field remains very far from level. Affirmative action, many liberals will accordingly argue, needs not only to remain on the books but to be vigorously enforced.

Affirmative action needs to continue, they contend, because established patterns of hiring too often constitute an "old boys" network, to the systematic disadvantage of outsiders in general and of minorities in particular. There is a need to make the selection processes more public, less under the control of the most powerful in society. As Amy Guttman has remarked, there "is a reason to be more suspicious of qualifications that are set by a small, privileged social group than of those that are widely scrutinized and agreed upon after deliberation by a broad spectrum of society."[32]

There is an irony here. For the very criticism that is leveled against "old boys'" networks for permitting established elites to conceal publicly indefensible choices under a veil of secrecy has still more force applied to affirmative action. The Achilles heel of affirmative action, so far as it entails preferential treatment, is precisely that it entails the adjudication of qualifications by a small, privileged social group, operating so far as possible without scrutiny, and certainly without the benefit of deliberation by a broad spectrum of society. The reason it must operate without scrutiny is that very different standards of evaluation for black and whites are *required* if the goals of affirmative action—an increase in the number of blacks admitted to certain universities and hired for certain jobs—are to be achieved. Consider college and university admissions. Purely as a matter of fact, even after correcting for every discernible form of error and bias, the differences between black and nonblack applicants in school grade point average and scores on standardized achievement tests remain large: on the most reliable estimates, over one standard deviation. It follows that even if the most active efforts are made to assure fair consideration for qualified minority applicants, if the same academic standards are used to evaluate black and white applicants—and if only academic qualifications are considered—the numbers of black students at academically outstanding universities will plummet.

We are well aware that *no university* uses academic qualifications alone to evaluate candidates for admission. Geographic, athletic, artistic factors, among many others, are taken into account, including whether the applicant's parents are contributing alumni, and it can be argued that it makes at least as much sense, from the point of view of both the larger society and of the individuals involved, to attend to considerations of race at least as closely as to those of geography or sports. We are also acutely aware that every formal measure of academic qualifications, whether in the form of school grades or standardized tests, is imperfect. It is not unreasonable to suggest that blacks, for altogether understandable reasons, are systematically vulnerable to getting lower scores than they deserve and, therefore, by placing less weight on test scores in the cases of blacks, we are actually admitting those who would have been improperly rejected had we relied only on their academic credentials.

Both of these arguments, if made publicly, could possibly be persuasive if affirmative action consisted only in giving a preference to a minority over a nonminority candidate when the two otherwise are closely comparable. But to accomplish what affirmative action is meant to accomplish—to boost significantly the admission or hiring rates of blacks where tests of achievement or aptitude are in standard use—it cannot be practiced at the margin. If blacks are to continue to be admitted in their current numbers to elite universities and professional schools, they routinely must be selected in the place of nonblacks whose formally relevant qualifications are strikingly superior. And *that* cannot be persuasively justified to citizens at large. The problem is not that citizens at large misunderstand what affirmative action is about and, if their misunderstandings were cleared up, they would support it. On the contrary, if they were to come to realize the full measure of the contemporary practice of affirmative action, their opposition in all likelihood would be even more intense.

In the end, there is an inescapable conflict between principle and practice. On the one side, there is a root belief that as a rule the person who is more qualified should be admitted to school or hired for a job over the person who is less qualified. On the other, given the magnitude of the differences between blacks and nonblacks in formally relevant qualifications, if blacks are to continue to be admitted in their current numbers to universities and professional schools, or hired and promoted in jobs involving standardized tests, they must be judged by different standards. And the consequence of this conflict is that the practice of affirmative action—what is actually done and how it is specifically accomplished—is not publicly defensible.

A route taken to deny that affirmative action poses a genuine dilemma for the liberal Democratic coalition is to appeal for the policy's reformulation, suggesting that it should now be class-based rather than race-based.[33] Principled arguments can be marshalled for a reformulation to provide increased opportunities for the economically disadvantaged, a disproportionate number of whom are black. But the idea that class-based affirmative action provides a way out is an illusion. From a purely practical point of view, favoring economically disadvantaged applicants will not only substantially reduce the number of blacks admitted but will also largely exclude the most qualified, since the most qualified blacks come overwhelmingly not from economically deprived but from comparatively well-off backgrounds. Moreover, class-based affirmative action is just as vulnerable as race-based to the root objection of selecting less qualified applicants in favor of more qualified ones. The unfairness is no less, and the resentment will be no less, if an A- student from a middle-class home is rejected to a state university in favor of a C+ student with an alcoholic single parent.

Continuing the commitment to affirmative action or giving it up—either choice risks splintering the Democratic party and liberalism. Not that the two are interchangeable. As a political party, the Democratic coalition has more opportunities for ambiguity and operates on many fronts simultaneously, only some of which have to do with principle. Liberalism has less freedom for maneuver. As a political philosophy, it has found its chief strength by issuing a moral call for public action to assist those who are worst off and to realize common ideas of fairness and equality. It is an irony, and may yet prove a tragedy, that the commitment to affirmative action that liberalism made out of this very sense of fairness may come to symbolize unfairness; and in the eyes not only of most of its opponents but also of many of its own adherents.

■

CHAPTER THREE

THE POWER OF PREJUDICE

How strong a grip does racial prejudice retain on the political thinking of white Americans? Viewed from the political left, racism remains all too common, and if it is not as overt or blatant as it once was, that is because whites are now more conscious that they should conceal their dislike of blacks. Viewed from the right, the alarm over racism is greatly exaggerated, and if prejudice has not entirely disappeared, it has lost its power to control whites' reactions to blacks. Liberals thus stress the continuing strength of racism, believing that conservatives underestimate the prejudice that persists in American society, while conservatives emphasize the marginality of racism, believing that liberals overestimate the prejudice that remains.

The conviction of each side that it knows the truth has blinded both. Contrary to the complacency of many conservatives, prejudice—as we will demonstrate—remains a significant force. There are fewer bigots, but that is far from saying there are only a few. Yet contrary to the skepticism of many liberals, most whites who say they think well of blacks are saying what they think, not just what they think they should say. There are, then, offsetting errors, with conservatives seeing what liberals overlook and liberals seeing what conservatives neglect.

But in addition to both of these errors, there is a third, unsuspected by conservatives and liberals alike. For a generation, commentators have taken for granted that racial prejudice is more powerful on the political right than on the left, and we, too, believed it at the start of our study. But in this as in several other respects, the evidence of our surveys has required us to change our minds.

It cannot be surprising that left and right disagree over the pervasiveness of prejudice in American popular culture. In spite of a seemingly endless stream of well-publicized commissions and studies over the last three decades, objective evidence on the actual frequency of race prejudice has been very nearly absent. Only at the start of the 1990s were three large-scale surveys of American attitudes toward blacks undertaken.[1]

Ours is the first analysis to draw on all three surveys. But we too must acknowledge, along with the skeptics, that a public opinion survey, however large in scale and systematic in character, only amounts to a record of words that people speak in response to questions put to them. If what is at issue is precisely whether or not to take people at their word, how can one ever determine the truth?

There is no way to demonstrate anything with absolute certainty in the study of public opinion. Yet we believe that some techniques can get closer to the truth than does the standard public opinion survey. In this chapter we will take advantage of number of new procedures made possible by computer-assisted interviewing. Each of these makes a contribution to our understanding of the nature and power of prejudice.

■ ■ ■

Do white Americans, when they think of "most blacks," see them as decent and hard-working, as dependable and law abiding, as the kind of people who make good neighbors? Or does their view of blacks continue to be hostile, derogatory? Do large numbers of white Americans perceive black Americans to be unintelligent, or undependable, or perhaps even dangerous? The Race and Politics Study conducted in 1991 attempted to answer these questions. Before asking whites what they think of blacks, we began with a brief introduction:

> Now I'll read a few words that people sometimes use to describe blacks. Of course, no word fits absolutely everybody, but, as I read each one, please tell me using a number from zero to ten how well you think it describes blacks as a group. If you think it's a VERY GOOD description of most blacks, give it a ten. If you feel a word is a VERY INACCURATE description of most blacks, give it a zero.

The interviewer then reads, one by one, a series of adjectives, asking each time how well, on a scale from 0 to 10, each adjective, describes "most blacks."[2]

Hostility to blacks can show itself in two ways—by agreement that blacks have negative characteristics, or alternatively, by denial that they have positive ones. Beginning with the latter, white Americans were asked whether "most blacks" are "friendly," "determined to succeed," "law abiding," "hardworking," "intelligent at school," "smart at everyday things," "good neighbors," "dependable," and "keep up their property." All of these descriptions are undemanding, amounting to no more than the modest praise people routinely pay those they encounter without complaint.

Given that it is virtually cost-free to say something nice about black Americans in the course of a public opinion interview, what is striking is how few white Americans actually do (see figure 9).[3] Apart from a general willingness of 3 out of 4 whites to describe blacks as "friendly"—surely as innocuous a positive quality as one can imagine—only a modest majority of whites are willing to attribute specific positive characteristics to most blacks. For example, only 50 to 60 percent are prepared to describe blacks as "smart at everyday things," "good neighbors," "hard-working," "intelligent at school," "dependable,"

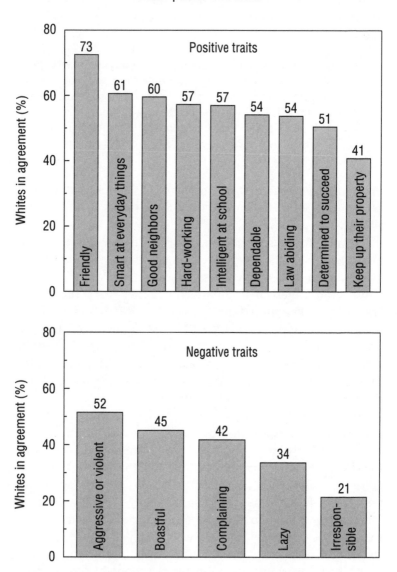

FIGURE 9
Whites' Agreement with Specific Positive or Negative
Descriptions of Blacks

Positive traits

Trait	%
Friendly	73
Smart at everyday things	61
Good neighbors	60
Hard-working	57
Intelligent at school	57
Dependable	54
Law abiding	54
Determined to succeed	51
Keep up their property	41

Negative traits

Trait	%
Aggressive or violent	52
Boastful	45
Complaining	42
Lazy	34
Irresponsible	21

Source: 1991 Race and Politics Study. Number of respondents ranges from 1,741 to 1,789.

"law abiding," or "determined to succeed." To be sure, declining to agree that most blacks are law abiding, for example, is not the same as denying that they are law abiding. Yet substantial numbers of whites, ranging from 25 to 60 percent, sit on the fence, not denying that blacks have a praiseworthy quality but not affirming it either. If it is reassuring that a majority of whites describe most blacks in positive terms, it is disturbing that the majority is far from overwhelming.

Declining to characterize black Americans in positive terms is one thing; publicly characterizing them in negative ones is quite another. To learn how commonplace negative evaluations are, we asked whether most blacks are "lazy," "boastful," "irresponsible," "complaining," or "aggressive or violent." Acknowledging that some negative characterizations of blacks are much more pervasive than others—the description of most blacks as "aggressive or violent" most of all—the point to emphasize is that the low point of agreement with negative descriptions of blacks is not very low at all. The least commonly endorsed negative characterization—that blacks are "irresponsible"—is endorsed by 1 out of every 5 whites—hardly a handful, judged either relatively or absolutely. The most commonly endorsed negative characterization—that blacks are "aggressive or violent"—is endorsed by 1 out of every 2, and very nearly as many declare that most blacks are "boastful" and "complaining." It is simply wrong to suppose that there is a shortage of white Americans willing to say, publicly, something overtly negative about black Americans.

Making a negative judgment of a group is not prejudice—otherwise everyone who ever made a critical remark about Jews would be an anti-Semite; prejudice consists of making negative judgments repeatedly, systematically. Let us therefore look at the readiness of white Americans systematically to attribute either negative or positive characteristics to black Americans (figure 10). On the one side, 35 percent of whites surveyed are prepared to attribute only three or fewer positive attributes (out of a possible nine) to most blacks. Still more grudgingly, 17 percent are willing to acknowledge only one positive attribute—or none at all. We should also point out that a still larger number of white Americans believe that black Americans have a great many positive qualities; 55 percent agree that five or more of the positive characteristics canvassed

FIGURE 10
Whites' Agreement with a Specific Number of Positive or Negative Descriptions of Blacks

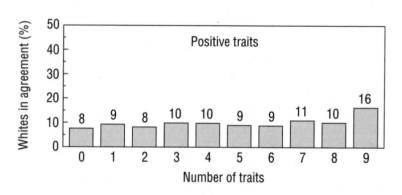

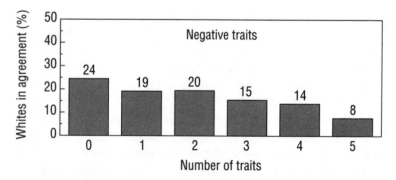

Source: 1991 Race and Politics Study. Number of respondents: positive traits, 1,735; negative trails, 1,721.

are a good description of most blacks, and 37 percent endorse seven or more of the positive attributes. As for the five negative characteristics surveyed, 22 percent of whites say that all, or nearly all, of them are a good description of most blacks. Yet 43 percent reject all, or nearly all, of the negative attributes as an inaccurate description of most blacks.

A sizeable number of white Americans, the survey results suggest, do not think well of black Americans, even if as many, or more, do. But there is an obvious asymmetry. It makes little sense to doubt that whites who say they dislike blacks mean what they say. It makes a good deal of sense to wonder if whites who say that they like blacks mean what *they* say.

It is on the rock of this reasonable doubt that current public opinion surveys have foundered. Every systematic study of long-term trends in American racial attitudes, without exception, has concluded that race prejudice has dramatically declined since the 1940s.[4] But the findings of public opinion polls no longer carry the authority they did a generation ago. Popular studies, without even troubling to ask white Americans what they think of black Americans, claim that white racism remains pervasive.[5] And they can be convincing to many because the persisting clash over issues of race has given new life to skepticism about the sincerity of whites' expressions of good will toward blacks.

To get a grip on whether whites who say they think well of blacks mean what they say, we carried out the Excuse Experiments. Quite simply, we wanted to find out how many whites who say they have a positive view of blacks would express a negative one, if they had a perfectly good excuse for doing so. Looking for situations where whites feel they can, with justification, express anxiety or anger about blacks, we focused on two—crime and welfare. The first Excuse Experiment centered on drugs. Respondents were told about a pair of men. To one half of the respondents, the men were described as white; to the other half, black. White or black, they were said to have been walking very near a house where the police knew drugs were being sold. The police subsequently searched them and found drugs. Respondents were then asked whether this search was reasonable or unreasonable and how confident they were that it was one or the other.[6]

The point of this Drug Search Experiment was to ensure that a randomly selected set of whites were able to justify a negative response to blacks on grounds completely unrelated to race. We wanted to hand them a socially acceptable reason to offer a negative evaluation of blacks in this situation and then see how many would take advantage of it. Accordingly, one half of the time the men (both the black pair and the white pair) were described as "using foul language" and the other half as "well-dressed and well-behaved." Respondents who were asked about two black men walking near where drugs were sold, and found to be in possession of drugs when subsequently searched, *and* using foul language, were perfectly positioned to say that the police search was reasonable. Whites who said they thought well of blacks, but really don't, could respond negatively to the blacks being searched, if they wished to, and with ease maintain that they thought that the search was reasonable not because the suspects were black but because their demeanor and the circumstances were suspicious.

Since our interest was in the sincerity of whites who said they thought well of blacks, we focused on the slice of respondents who previously reported having positive attitudes toward blacks. Specifically, we looked at those who said they believed blacks to be "law abiding" and did not believe them to be "aggressive or violent,"[7] since the issues raised in the Drug Search Experiment had to do with antisocial and criminal behavior. The question, then, is this: Having put an excuse in the hands of whites who said they thought well of blacks, allowing them legitimately to respond negatively to blacks, would we find that they were likely to take advantage of it?

Antisocial behavior, according to our respondents, *was* a credible consideration to justify a police search. Consider the case of white suspects (see figure 11). If white suspects were using foul language, 66 percent of white respondents judged a police search reasonable, as opposed to 47 percent who judged a search reasonable when the white suspects were "well-dressed and "well-behaved." The crux of the matter, however, is whether black suspects were judged differently by white respondents who said they think well of blacks but who had the suspects' antisocial behavior as an excuse for expressing their prejudice.

What we found was that whites attached the same weight— no more, no less—to using foul language in the case of blacks suspects as white suspects. If black suspects were using foul language, 60 percent of white respondents thought that a police search was reasonable, a percentage statistically identical to that for white suspects. Similarly, 50 percent thought a search was reasonable when black suspects were well-behaved, as compared with 47 percent for white suspects—again virtually identical. In short, these results suggest that whites who said they thought well of blacks meant what they said; even when they had a socially acceptable excuse to think badly of blacks, they did not take advantage of it.

The idea behind the Welfare Mother Experiment, the second of the Excuse Experiments, was again to put respondents into a position where they could express negativity toward a black, if they wished to, and yet claim credibly that their reason for a negative response had nothing to do with the fact the person was black. In this second experiment, a welfare mother was described as in her early thirties, with a ten-year-old child and a record of having been on welfare for the past year. For half of the respondents (chosen randomly), she was described as black, and for the other half she was described as white. In addition, one half of the white welfare mothers were described

FIGURE 11
Excuse Experiments

The Drug Search Experiment

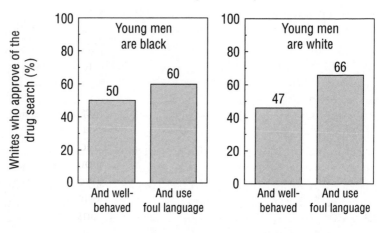

The Welfare Mother Experiment

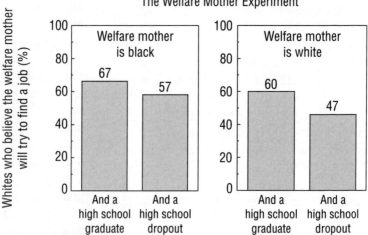

Source: 1991 Race and Politics Study. Number of respondents ranges from 135 to 190. Tests of statistical significance: person described as white versus black, t = 0.73, p < 0.464; well behaved/uses foul language, t = 3.04, p < 0.002; black vs. white using foul language, t = 1.05, p < 0.295; person is described as white vs. black, t = 2.10, p < 0.036; high school graduate/dropout, t = 2.85, p < 0.004; black vs. white on high school dropout, t = 0.25, p < 0.800.

as "a high school dropout" and the other half as "a high school graduate." These same two descriptions were applied to the black welfare mothers.

The test question about the welfare mother was put as follows:

> How likely do you think it is that she will really try hard to find a job in the next year—very likely, somewhat likely, somewhat unlikely, or not at all likely?

The idea was to make it easy, not hard, for respondents to express a negative judgment. It was not necessary to declare that the woman on welfare would never try to look for work; it was only necessary to doubt whether she would really try hard to find a job in the course of the coming year.

Since the specific issues raised in the experiment had to do with a willingness to work hard and to demonstrate a sense of responsibility, we looked specifically at those respondents who had previously reported having a positive attitude about blacks' being "dependable" and "hardworking" and not being "lazy" and "irresponsible."[8] The question was: Did they mean what they said about blacks?

The characterization of the mother as a high school dropout *was*, according to our respondents, an acceptable justification for doubts about women on welfare. In the case of a white mother on welfare, 60 percent of white respondents believed that a high school graduate would try hard to find a job and get off welfare, whereas only 47 percent believed she would try if she was a high school dropout (figure 11). But did they attach more weight to the same piece of damaging information if it was applied to a black mother on welfare?

For white respondents, being a dropout was not a good sign. But it was no more of a bad sign if the dropout was black rather than white. In the case of a black high school dropout, 57 percent of whites thought she would try hard to get a job, whereas 67 percent thought a black high school graduate would try hard. Thus, whites who said they thought well of blacks, confronting one who had failed to graduate from high school, did not take special advantage of her being a dropout to respond negatively to her.

We are not suggesting that every white American who says he thinks well of black Americans does so: of course, some will say something nice about blacks in public opinion interviews even though they think badly of them. What we are saying is that, if whites consistently are positive in the views they express of blacks in general, as large numbers of them now are, that is the way they act—even when they are perfectly positioned to do otherwise.

■　■　■

It is important that fewer whites think ill of blacks than they did a half a century ago. But because there are fewer bigots does not mean that there are only a few. We want, accordingly, to turn to the principal question of interest to commentators on race. How powerful a role does race prejudice now play in shaping the political thinking of whites about issues of race?

It has been a common presumption that white Americans resist a range of policies to achieve racial equality not because they are compelled to object to government action in behalf of blacks on some ground of principle but because they still, irrationally and intensely, dislike black Americans—and disliking them, they dislike governmental policies designed to help them. In order to believe this, it is not necessary to think that racial prejudice is the only factor at work, nor even that it necessarily remains the most powerful one at work. It is necessary only to believe that prejudice continues to play a significant role in propping up opposition to efforts to achieve racial equality. Speaking for ourselves, this seems on its face a reasonable view, and to take any other position—whether claiming that prejudice no longer exercises any influence whatever or of asserting that it alone exerts an influence—seems unreasonable.

What does it mean to say that racial prejudice continues to exert a significant influence on the political thinking of white Americans on issues of race? Expressed in quantitative terms, it comes to this. The stronger the influence of prejudice, the more readily predictable are people's positions on policies dealing with blacks, given knowledge of their feelings toward blacks. Exactly how predictable their positions are can be expressed in terms of a correlation coefficient: the larger the magnitude of the coefficient, the greater the degree of predictability, with a coefficient of 1.0 indicating perfect predictability; the smaller the magnitude of the coefficient, the lower the degree of predictability, with a coefficient of 0 indicating a complete absence of predictability.

By way of orientation, table 4 shows how predictable the positions of whites are on an array of issues of race, given knowledge of their feelings toward blacks. Clearly, there is a relation: the more whites dislike blacks, the more likely they are to oppose, for example, government programs to help blacks get jobs or to see that blacks get fair treatment in getting jobs. But the most striking feature of these figures is how small they are. The coefficients range from 0.05 to 0.28, but typically they run about 0.16. These values are significantly different from zero, but they are conspicuous for their modesty.

It has been difficult for us, as researchers, to accept that the impact of racial prejudice on policy preferences, although certainly detectable, is so small. Although we have always been prepared to acknowledge that other factors are at work, in our Race and Politics Study we started from a presumption of many years' standing that racial prejudice played a major role in shaping the political thinking of white Americans. At first, we supposed the magnitude of prejudice's impact was being suppressed by technical quandaries of measurement. In a series of

TABLE 4
Correlation between Racial Prejudice and Support
for Racial Policies among Whites

Policy	Correlation[a]
1991 Race and Politics Study	
Government spending on programs to help blacks get more jobs	.20
Fighting discrimination against blacks in jobs	.16
Job quotas for blacks	.16
Welfare spending	.12
Preferential admissions to universities for blacks	.05
1990 General Social Survey	
Government responsibility to help blacks	.22
Spending to help blacks	.18
1992 National Election Study	
Preferential admissions to universities for blacks	.17
Programs to help blacks	.22
Government spending to help blacks	.28
Preference in hiring for blacks	.12
School integration	.15
Welfare spending	.11

Number of respondents: RAP, from 528 to 1,708; GSS, from 479 to 1,031; NES, from 1,225 to 17,19.
a. p<.001 level for all items.

studies in which we experimented with different methods of measurement, however, the impact of prejudice on political thinking was never larger than the values shown in this table, and often it was smaller.

In an effort to make as certain as possible that our results were reliable, we turned to the General Social Survey and the National Election Study and for each calculated equivalent measures of the impact of racial prejudice on political thinking. The actual questions in the two studies measuring both racial policy preferences and racial prejudice in detail differ markedly from our own, and indeed in some respects from each other. But the lesson of all three studies consistently came up the same: there is a range of values, from essentially 0.1 to about 0.3, depending on the specific issue and wording of the question, but the coefficients never are very large, and typically are quite small.[9] The conclusion to draw, these results suggest, is that although the influence of racial prejudice on the political thinking of white Americans continues to be detectible, prejudice is very far from a dominating factor in the contemporary politics of race.

Yet this finding conflicted with our own intuitive sense of the continuing importance of racial prejudice in shaping the thinking of white Americans. Finding it impossible to dismiss the results of the objective analysis, and equally impossible to dismiss our subjective sense that racial prejudice was not a spent force, we reasoned a way out of this dilemma. Even if racial prejudice was no longer a primary force in the public as a whole, it could remain a major factor in politically significant parts of it.

In an effort to see how racial animus might still exert a politically significant influence, we undertook to explore the interconnections of prejudice, political ideology, and the party system.

Broadly, the agreed view of analysts and commentators on the political impact of race prejudice has run as follows. Po-

litical conservatism and race prejudice tend to be tied together. Conservatism as a political outlook is marked by an
apprehension about political and social change in general and
tends, in consequence, to stress social conformity and political
authority. The intuition is that conservatism in politics should
therefore appeal to people who out of prejudice reject others
who are different in appearance or outlook.[10] That is, racists
should be disproportionately likely to embrace conservatism,
although it does not follow that most conservatives are racists.

Once kept in the obscurity of the wings of American politics,
the issue of race moved to center stage in the early 1960s, in
large measure thanks to the success of the civil rights movement in dramatizing the violence and hardships suffered by
blacks in the South.[11] Having again become salient, the issue
of race served as a fulcrum for a realignment of the party
system. With the 1964 presidential contest of Barry Goldwater
and Lyndon Johnson, the Republican party, which had been
the champion of racial liberalism under Lincoln, became the
party of racial conservatism. Conversely, the Democratic party,
which had been a bulwark of racial conservatism, became the
champion of racial liberalism.

Race did not, all on its own, produce this realignment of
American politics, but cleavages over racial policies have come
to coincide with, rather than cut across, cleavages of both
ideology and partisanship. On issue after issue—from government spending to improve the social and economic position
of blacks, through regulatory oversight of employment practices, through busing and affirmative action—the political left,
that is, liberals and the Democratic party, have come to champion the use of government on behalf of blacks, and the
political right, conservatives and the Republican party, have as
consistently stood in opposition.[12]

It is only natural that this overlap of political conservatism and opposition to government programs to assist blacks
should suggest to many observers, whether they are them-

selves on the political left or not, that racial prejudice plays its largest role on the political right. Conservatism and prejudice, according to this view, politically reinforce each other, both encouraging whites to oppose public policies to help blacks, whatever the policies' specific objective or mode of implementation.

This view of prejudice as exerting its force chiefly on the political right we call the "prejudice-on-the-right" thesis, and it has an important kernel of truth. Table 5 lays out the relation between ideological orientation and dislike of blacks, based on results from the National Election Study, the General Social Survey, and the Race and Politics Study. One can see that the more conservative the respondent is, the higher his level of prejudice, and although the relation is not very strong, it is consistently true for all three studies. In short, racial prejudice is more common on the political right than on the political left.

But the cleavage over race goes deeper on the political left. As a number of political commentators have observed, for a generation the Democratic coalition has found itself strained by the issue of race.[13] The eruption of race riots in the mid 1960s and of mass protests over busing in the late 60s began the process of polarization on the left. The issue of crime became linked, on the one side, with race as violent crime exploded in the inner cities, and on the other, with liberalism as it spearheaded a revolution in rights, including the rights of those accused of crime. Demands for racial reparation came to be seen as one plank among many in the left's condemnation of American society's racism. To many, spiraling expenditures for welfare seemed to go hand in hand with a surge in problems for the black family, while for a decade and more opinion on the left insisted that blacks' becoming worse off was the larger society's fault and that to suggest otherwise was "to blame the victim." The biracial civil rights coalition splintered in response to the pressure for black separatism and under the strain of black anti-Semitism. All of these rifts were

TABLE 5
Correlation between Political Ideology and
Race Prejudice among Whites

Survey	Correlation[a]
1991 Race and Politics Study	.13
1990 General Social Survey	.09
1992 National Election Study	.14

Prejudice is scored from low to high, political ideology from liberal to conservative. Number of respondents: RAP, 1,102; GSS, 1,216; NES, 1,550.
a. p<.001 for all items.

exacerbated by race-conscious programs like affirmative action. Although they had originated under a Republican president and were initially subjected to criticism from civil rights organizations, positions soon reversed in the dance of politics: liberalism embraced and dramatically expanded the scope of race-conscious remedies, and reaped the resentment and anger that came in their wake.

Liberals and the Democratic coalition have operated under a severe strain for the last two decades because of the new politics of race, very much to the advantage of the right and the Republican coalition. Most visibly at the presidential level, but increasingly at the local and state level, the argument is that Republicans have gained votes by taking advantage of a complex of issues in which resentment over race, rights, and welfare is a prominent element.

When political conservatives who dislike blacks are asked whether a new government program should be set up to expand job training for blacks, they face an easy choice. The answer is no, there should not be yet another government program to benefit blacks. They may come to that decision on the basis of their political outlook or on the basis of their negative feelings toward blacks, but either way the outcome is the same. Imagine, by comparison, whites who are politically conservative but who like blacks and feel sympathetic toward them. How should they respond to a proposal to establish a new government-run program to assist blacks? Obviously, just so far as they are conservative, they should oppose it. But does it follow that, just so far as they truly do feel sympathy and a positive regard for blacks, they should support this new program? After all, it is being set up in order to help blacks, and if they genuinely do like and identify with blacks, shouldn't they back it notwithstanding the fact that they are conservatives?

So it may seem, at first glance. But it only seems so if the merits of the program are judged from a liberal perspective. For a conservative, the fact that the adoption of a government program is urged in order to help blacks is hardly proof that it will, if adopted, actually help them. On the contrary, from a conservative perspective, establishment of another Washington-run jobs program may seem a museum-quality specimen of an approach to public policy that not only has not improved the welfare of those it is supposed to help but has arguably left them worse off. It follows that when conservatives are asked either to support or oppose another government-run jobs program to assist blacks, just insofar as they truly are conservative, they face an easy choice, however they feel about blacks.

But if the question of whether a new government jobs program for blacks should be established is easy for conservatives, it can be hard for many liberals precisely because of how many of them feel toward blacks. Although fewer liberals (as compared to conservatives) score as racially prejudiced, this does not mean that only a few liberals are racially prejudiced, as we have just seen. In the Race and Politics Study, for example, approximately 1 out of every 4 liberals scores in the upper third of negative evaluations of blacks, as compared with about 1 out of every 3 conservatives. And liberals who dislike blacks come up against a hard choice about government programs to help blacks just insofar as their feelings about blacks collide with their view—as liberals—as to what government ought to do in behalf of the disadvantaged. On the one side, just so far they are genuinely liberal, they are under pressure to favor government programs to benefit blacks; on the other side, just so far as they sincerely dislike blacks, they should be inclined to oppose them.

What does this reasoning imply, if it is right, about the role of prejudice in contemporary American politics? As a basis for deciding whether to support government activism in behalf of blacks, how whites feel about blacks should be a consideration of secondary importance if they are on the political right: just so far as they are committed to conservatism as a political philosophy, they have at hand a relevant reason for opposition, however they feel about blacks. By contrast, if they are on the political left, how whites feel about blacks should be a consideration of primary importance: just so far as they genuinely dislike blacks, they should be reluctant to support programs that as liberals they otherwise should welcome. The consequence, if this is what is going on, is ironic: where prejudice is weakest, that is, on the political left, its political impact may be strongest, that is, most capable of bolstering opposition to government efforts to assist blacks.

Does racial prejudice more powerfully shape the political thinking of those on the left than those on the right? In figure 12 we chart the support for specific racial policies as a function of how racially prejudiced whites are. The solid line represents strong liberals; the dotted line represents strong conservatives.[14] If the line is flat as it moves from left to right, it means that differences in the degree to which people are prejudiced make no difference in the likelihood of their supporting government help for blacks. On the other hand, the more the line falls as it moves from left to right, the more powerful racial prejudice is.

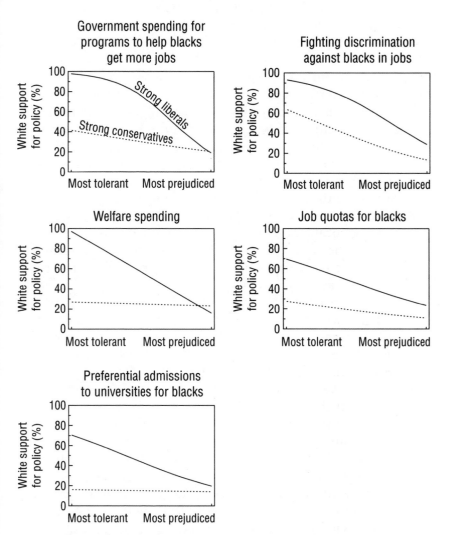

FIGURE 12
White Support for Government Programs to Help Blacks, by
Ideology and Level of Prejudice

Source: 1991 Race and Politics Study. Prejudice ranges from most tolerant 1% to the most
prejudiced 1% of whites.

The crucial question is whether prejudice exercises a stronger influence in shaping the political thinking on issues of race of political liberals than of conservatives. As figure 12 shows, for conservatives, prejudice makes only a slight difference in the likelihood of their supporting government help for blacks. The dotted line is uniformly low and essentially flat, indicating that conservatives tend to oppose each of these government programs regardless of how positively or negatively they feel toward blacks.

The results for liberals differ dramatically, as illustrated by the drop in the solid line. If their feelings toward blacks are positive, they are overwhelmingly likely to support government assistance for blacks—the odds are approximately 8 out of 10 that liberals with the most positive feelings toward blacks will favor government help for blacks. But the more negative liberals' feelings are toward blacks, the less likely they are to support their very own policy agenda on issues of race. Indeed, strong liberals who are prejudiced are just as likely as strong conservatives, whether prejudiced or not, to oppose government programs designed to assist blacks.

We have tried in as many ways as we can conceive to see if these findings hold up. One of these tests is to turn the focus from a comparison of liberals and conservatives to a comparison of Democrats and Republicans. The basic logic of the argument remains the same. So far as Republicans take the political point of view of the right, it should not especially matter to them how they feel toward blacks, since whether they feel positively or negatively toward them, they have an immediately relevant reason to oppose government programs of assistance for them. By contrast, how Democrats feel toward blacks should count for a good deal more. So far as they take the political point of view of the left, they ought to support government assistance for blacks, but so far as they dislike blacks, they should wish instead to oppose assistance for blacks.

Figure 13 plots the impact of racial prejudice among strong

FIGURE 13
White Support for Government Programs to Help Blacks, by Partisanship and Level of Prejudice

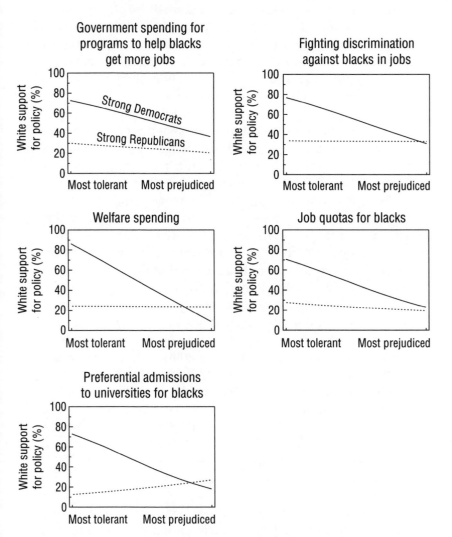

Source: 1991 Race and Politics Study. Prejudice ranges from most tolerant 1% to the most prejudiced 1% of whites.

Democrats (solid line) and strong Republicans (dotted line). Again, the steeper the falling line, the bigger the impact of racial prejudice; the flatter the line, the smaller its impact. As a glance will show, the line falls off dramatically in the case of Democrats, indicating that their feelings toward blacks have a strong influence on the positions they take on racial policies. In the case of Republicans, however, it is essentially flat, indicating that their feelings toward blacks have little influence on the positions they take on racial policies.

It is important to underline the consistency of these empirical results. We have looked at a whole array of racial issues, and whenever racial prejudice is a force shaping the political thinking of whites, it is always a significantly more important force shaping the thinking of those on the left than the thinking of those on the right. It is, moreover, not a matter of focusing only on racial issues, such as affirmative action, that are uncommonly controversial or divisive. Instead we have concentrated also on racial policies in the mainstream of political argument, such as federal job training programs for blacks, federal antidiscrimination programs, and welfare.

We are aware that there is an inescapable element of chance to the results from any single study, and therefore we have examined the General Social Survey and the National Election Study in addition to the Race and Politics Study. The results from the three studies could easily have differed because the specific measures of racial prejudice and of racial policies differ, occasionally in major ways. Yet, the results from all three studies consistently demonstrate that the impact of whites' feelings toward blacks more powerfully shapes the political thinking of those on the political left than those on the political right (see appendix figures 1 and 2).

One objection that might be raised to our finding that prejudice is more politically powerful on the left than on the right is that the ideological labels ordinary citizens pin on themselves can be misleading, notoriously so.[15] Merely because an ordinary citizen describes his political outlook as liberal does not necessarily mean that he consistently takes liberal positions on the major issues of the day, let alone that he has any grasp of the principles of liberalism. On the contrary, many who describe themselves as liberal in fact take up positions on the conservative side of major issues, just as many who categorize themselves as conservative line up on the liberal side.[16] Perhaps, then, prejudice only seems to have a greater impact on liberals' political thinking because they are not really liberals. They want, for whatever reason and perhaps for no better reason than habit, to see themselves—or to be seen by others—as being liberal. Once they were loyal Democrats. But as the issues of crime, welfare, busing, taxation, and the revolution of rights came increasingly to the fore, they migrated to the right. In the process, they have become, in everything but name, conservatives, siding with the right on the major issues of the day and swinging over to the Republican side, if not always openly, then certainly in the privacy of the ballot box.

It is surely possible that many whites who dislike blacks are liberal in name only. And if the political currents have already pulled them from left to right, if they are conservative in all but name, then the apparently stronger impact of prejudice on the left may be an illusion. It is crucial, then, to determine whether liberals who dislike blacks really are liberal in every area except racial politics. Because of the importance of getting to the bottom of this, we are going to explore two quite different kinds of evidence—one orthodox and direct, the other novel and indirect.

Beginning with direct evidence, if the question is whether liberals who dislike blacks are really liberals, then the most important thing to check is whether they take liberal stands on public policies that do not involve race. The issue of race has become a strand of American liberalism, but it is far from the only one and is not necessarily the most central. To take account of the principal strands of liberal belief, we canvassed views on a range of aspects of inequality and governmental activism, including government spending to reduce unemployment, providing medical insurance for the unemployed, repealing tax breaks for the rich, and narrowing the gap between rich and poor. Moreover, to take account of the possibility that liberals who dislike blacks, even if politically liberal on bread-and-butter issues, may be conservative on social issues, we additionally examined their views on abortion and prayer in public schools.

The more liberal the position people take on each of these issues, the higher the bars in figure 14. If liberals who are racially prejudiced are liberal in name only, then their views on all these issues, instead of paralleling those of liberals who are racially tolerant, should resemble those of conservatives, however they feel toward blacks. But their views on bread and butter issues of government activism are very nearly indistinguishable from those of their fellow liberals. Liberals who dislike blacks are just as likely to favor medical care for the unemployed and just as likely to support repeal of tax breaks for the rich as liberals who feel positively toward blacks. A few differences are detectible on a few issues. For example, liberals who dislike blacks are slightly more likely to oppose abortion and slightly less likely to favor narrowing the gap between rich and poor. But these slight differences are of no consequence politically. Liberals who are prejudiced against blacks not only do *not* line up on the conservative side of any of these issues, including the hot-button social issues of prayer in the public schools and abortion, but on issue after issue they predominantly take the liberal side. In short, liberals who dislike blacks are not liberal in name only: they are liberal *and* racially prejudiced.

Choosing a position on issues of race, it follows, should be difficult for them. Their political convictions should pull them in one direction, in favor of programs to assist the worst off;

FIGURE 14
White Liberals' Support for Liberal Policies, by Level of Prejudice

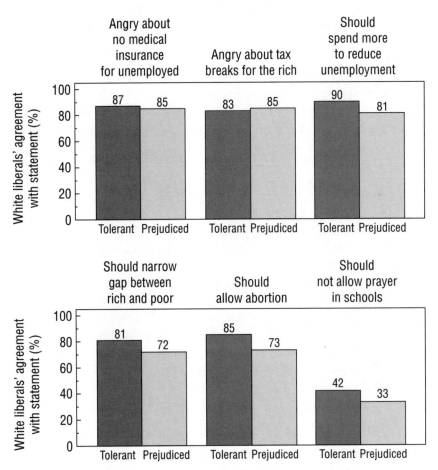

Source: 1991 Race and Politics Study. Number of respondents ranges from 56 to 125.

their racial prejudice should pull them in the opposite direction, against government assistance for blacks. By contrast, liberals who feel positively toward blacks ought to be free of cross-pressures. Their politics and their feelings toward blacks work hand in hand. They should want to support liberal programs on issues of race, both because they really are liberal and because they genuinely feel a sense of positive regard for blacks.

The reasoning is plausible. But is it right? It is by no means obvious how to establish objectively if liberals who are racially prejudiced are being pulled in opposing directions. It is not as though, because they are pulled in opposing political directions, they split the difference between them. In fact, in terms of the positions they take, instead of choosing a middle ground between liberal and conservative poles, we have seen that the views of liberals who dislike blacks are virtually indistinguishable from those of conservatives who like blacks—both oppose public policies that assist blacks. Nor will asking them directly whether they feel conflicted manifestly do. If some liberals oppose liberal programs on issues of race because they dislike blacks, why suppose that they would openly admit this?

Thinking about this, we reasoned that, although we cannot rely directly on what liberals say, we may perhaps take advantage of how long they take to say it. If liberals who dislike blacks are indeed being pulled in two opposing directions, then when asked to take a stand on a racial policy, should they not hesitate?

We mean quite literally hesitate. They should, if they are conflicted, take just an extra fraction of time before responding to a question, the sort of brief pause that in the ordinary course of an interview or conversation would not be noticed at all, before committing themselves to a position on a policy aimed at helping blacks. Accordingly, a special experiment was conducted, taking advantage of the clock embedded in the computers controlling the interview schedule. Everyone was asked their view of government assistance for a disadvantaged group: however, for one half of respondents, on a random basis, the group to be assisted was "blacks and minorities"; for the other half of respondents, the group was "new immigrants from Europe." As an additional feature of this experiment, interviewers were trained to strike a special key on their computer keyboards to mark the time when they finished reading the target question and again to mark the time when the respondent began to answer. Since we wanted to be able to spot not merely an embarrassingly obvious delay but also a subtle hesitation, response time was measured in hundredths of a second.[17]

If liberals who dislike blacks are indeed being pulled in one direction by their liberalism and in another by their racial prejudice, then they should take detectably longer to begin to answer a question about whether blacks should be helped than to respond to the same question about whether a nonblack group should be helped. And indeed they do. When whites are to benefit from government assistance, liberals who dislike blacks took just over a second to start their responses (see figure 15). By contrast, when blacks are to benefit, they took just over 2.5 seconds to start. There is, then, a hesitation of about 1.5 seconds when blacks are the beneficiaries named in the question. This difference, although it would have gone unnoticed in the normal course of things, easily meets tests of statistical significance. It demonstrates that liberal respondents are indeed pulled in conflicting directions by their political convictions and their racial prejudice. But, as we have seen, they overwhelmingly resolve this conflict in favor of their prejudice rather than their politics.

Let us, however, try to challenge our finding that prejudice is more politically powerful on the left from the opposite direction. Instead of questioning whether liberals who dislike blacks really are liberal, let us instead ask whether conservatives who say they like blacks really do like blacks. Per-

FIGURE 15
Reaction Time of Prejudiced White Liberals to Questions
about Government Help for the Poor

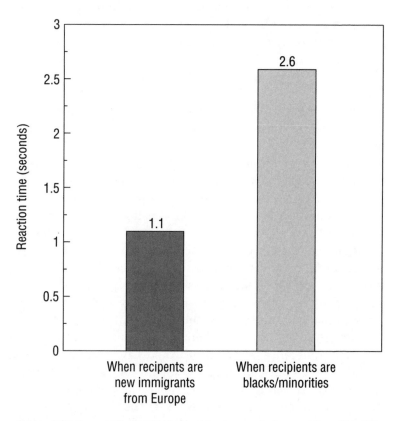

Source: 1991 Race and Politics Study. Number of respondents ranges from 25 to 34
Tests of statistical significance: black/new immigrant, $t = 1.91$, $p < 0.031$, one-tailed.

haps conservatives who report that they feel positively toward blacks are only saying what they think they should say. Asked to take a stand on an issue of race, they will oppose, just so far as they are conservative, a proposal to boost government spending for job training programs. And just so far as they say that they like blacks—but do not mean what they say—they will oppose assistance for blacks without compunction. The result: there will be no connection between the actual stands that conservatives take on issues of race and the feelings they publicly express about blacks.

The crucial question, then, is whether or not conservatives who say they feel positively toward blacks really do. Since obviously we cannot ask them directly whether they are being sincere or merely dissembling—if they are not telling the truth to one question, why believe they will be truthful in response to any other?—we need a disguised test. Hence the Government Dependency Experiment.

The idea behind the Government Dependency Experiment is this. Think of a judgment that conservatives are accustomed to make—for example, that too many people take advantage of government assistance, preferring the security of public help to the challenge of standing on their own two feet. Just so far as people are conservative, they should find this suggestion credible and feel comfortable in saying so. From their point of view, after all, to warn of the dangers of dependency on government assistance is a mark of a conservative outlook, not evidence of meanness of spirit. To tell if conservatives who say they like blacks mean what they say, we can then set up a test, sometimes asking them whether blacks, and sometimes whether nonblacks, take advantage of government assistance. If we manage the details well, and if conservatives who say they like blacks indeed mean what they say, then at a minimum they should be evenhanded racially, neither more nor less likely to say that blacks take advantage of government programs than nonblacks.

The Government Dependency Experiment consists of three experimental conditions, identical in every respect except for the group said to be exploiting government assistance. In the first—or "poverty"—version of the problem, a randomly selected set of respondents is asked to respond to the statement:

Most poor people these days would rather take assistance from the government than make it on their own through hard work.

Then, for comparison, we created a second—or "race"—version of the problem, with one third of respondents asked whether they agree or disagree with the following statement:

Most blacks these days would rather take assistance from the government than make it on their own through hard work.

Finally, for reasons we shall explain in a moment, we created a third—or "combined"—condition joining considerations of both race and poverty, with the final third of respondents asked whether they agree or disagree with the following statement:

Most poor blacks these days would rather take assistance from the government than make it on their own through hard work.

The crucial issue is how conservatives who say they like blacks react to blacks as compared to poor people. If their reactions are not evenhanded, if they are more likely to say that blacks take advantage of government assistance, then their claim to think well of blacks is likely false. On the other hand, if they are evenhanded, neither more nor less likely to respond adversely to blacks as compared with poor people, then the claim that they mean what they say when they say they think well of blacks is credible.

In fact, as figure 16 shows, they go well beyond being simply evenhanded. Instead of being *more* likely to characterize blacks as welfare dependents, racially tolerant conservatives are significantly *less* likely to do so. This is a result worth underlining.

FIGURE 16
Government Dependency Experiment

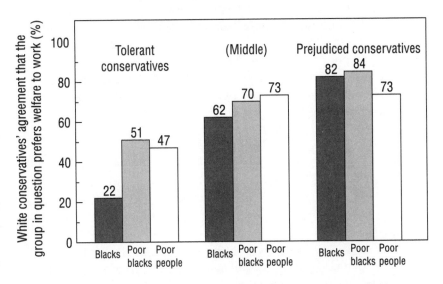

Source: 1991 Race and Politics Study. Number of respondents ranges from 33 to 61. Tests of statistical significance: racially tolerant, poor people vs. blacks, $t = 2.69$, $p < 0.01$; racially tolerant, poor people vs. poor blacks, $t = 0.45$, $p < 0.65$.

The notion that many people would prefer to take advantage of government handouts rather than stand on their own two feet is a staple of conservative thought. Yet conservatives who say they feel positively toward blacks are distinctively reluctant to apply it to blacks, evidence that they do not just say they like blacks but actually do.

Yet, perhaps their reluctance to characterize blacks as exploiting government assistance, rather than being evidence of good will toward blacks, is merely the result of a reluctance to say something negative about blacks publicly. The Government Dependency Experiment was designed to get around this quandary. Instead of just contrasting reactions to "blacks" and "poor people," it includes a third comparison, "poor blacks." If conservatives who say they like blacks respond positively to blacks in the Government Dependency Experiment only because they are unwilling to respond negatively to them publicly, then they should similarly be unwilling to respond negatively to poor blacks. On the other hand, if they are being sincere, then just as they said that the poor take advantage of government assistance, so they should say that poor blacks exploit it.

In fact, looking at their reactions to "poor blacks," we can see that they are not in fact debarred from saying something negative about blacks. On the contrary, they are just as likely to say that poor blacks take advantage of government help as do poor people in general, which is strong evidence that when conservatives respond positively to blacks, they mean what they say.

Conservatives who feel positively toward blacks, the evidence so far suggests, nevertheless tend to oppose government policies designed to help blacks, such as government-run job training programs, because programs of this stripe conflict with their principles as conservatives. But if they were presented with a policy designed to help blacks which does *not* conflict with their conservative principles, and if they genuinely do feel positively toward blacks, wouldn't they support it?

Consider the issue of integration. It is one thing for conservatives to object, on principle, to increasing federal government spending for social welfare programs; quite another for them to object, on principle, to facilitating racial integration. Specific ways of achieving integration—for example, by establishing a federal bureaucracy to promote it—may have little appeal for conservatives, even if they are genuinely sympathetic toward blacks. But unless they will give a positive showing of support for integration in some circumstances, then surely it is fair to question whether they do genuinely feel positively toward blacks.

To see to what extent, and in what ways, conservatives will support racial integration, the Integration Experiment was carried out. In this experiment, three different methods of achieving racial integration are considered, varying in the amount and type of government involvement. To avoid contaminating the response to one method by having first brought up another, only one approach to integration, selected on a random basis, is presented to each respondent.

In all cases respondents were asked if they favor or oppose programs to encourage blacks to buy houses in white suburbs.[18] To capture views about integration through nongovernmental agencies, 1 out of 3 respondents was asked if they favor or oppose:

> programs set up by religious and business groups that encourage blacks to buy homes in white suburbs.

To gauge views about government-encouraged but not government-mandated integration, 1 out of 3 respondents was asked if they favor or oppose:

> the government putting its weight behind programs to encourage blacks to buy homes in white suburbs.

Finally, to estimate views about programs for integration that are both government-led and government-funded, 1 out of 3 respondents was asked if they favor or oppose:

> government subsidized housing to encourage blacks to buy homes in white suburbs.

If conservatives who say they like blacks truly do, how should they react to these three programs to achieve integration? At a minimum, they should support integration achieved through nongovernmental agencies; and, moreover, they should do so to an extent that distinguishes them clearly from conservatives who dislike blacks. Indeed, they should resemble liberals. Looking at the results from the Integration Experiment, we can see that this is in fact so (figure 17). Conservatives who like blacks are significantly more likely to support programs to achieve racial integration through nongovernmental groups than conservatives who dislike blacks, and they do not differ significantly in their support for these programs from liberals who like blacks.

By contrast, when integration is to be promoted through government-subsidized housing programs, conservatives who like blacks are as likely to be opposed as those who dislike blacks. When integration is to be promoted by a compromise position, with government encouraging but not mandating it, conservatives who like blacks are twice as likely to support it as those who dislike blacks; they do not significantly differ in their level of support from liberals, including even liberals who feel positively toward blacks.

There is, then, evidence in two forms that conservatives who say they like blacks mean what they say: on the one hand, they do not respond negatively to blacks even when their conservative outlook provides a natural justification for their doing so; and they distinctively support policies to assist blacks when the policy does not conflict with their conservative principles.

■　■　■

Our finding that racial prejudice on the left is more politically powerful than on the right has implications worth consideration. Think about the capacity of the political left and right to command the allegiance of their respective supporters on questions of race. By way of a specific illustration, look at the positions liberals and conservatives take on whether to increase government spending to combat black unemployment (figure 18). There are four groups on which we want to con-

FIGURE 17
Integration Experiment

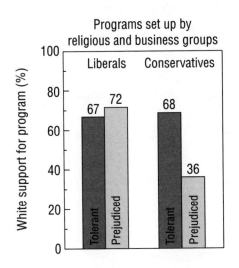

Programs set up by religious and business groups

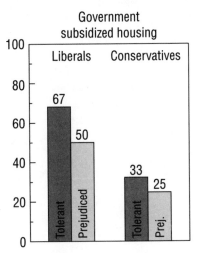

Government subsidized housing

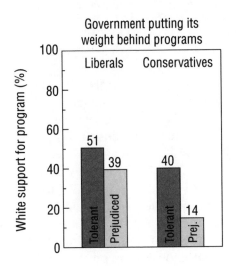

Government putting its weight behind programs

Source: 1991 Race and Politics Study. Number of respondents ranges from 13 to 55.

FIGURE 18
White Opposition to Government Spending to Increase Black Employment, by Ideology and Level of Prejudice

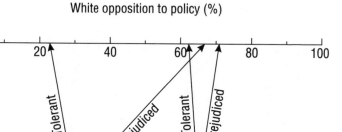

White opposition to policy (%)

Source: 1991 Race and Politics Study. Number of respondents ranges from 24 to 59. Tests for statistical significance, comparing groups: tolerant liberals vs. prejudiced liberals, t = 3.62, p < 0.001; tolerant liberals vs. tolerant conservatives, t = 4.21, p < 0.001; tolerant liberals vs. prejudiced conservatives, t = 5.00, p < 0.001.

centrate: liberals who are racially tolerant, liberals who are racially prejudiced, conservatives who are racially tolerant, and conservatives who are racially prejudiced. To give some sense of the politics of racial prejudice, we have first lined up these groups in terms of their overall political direction, with liberals on the left and conservatives on the right. Then we have drawn arrows beginning from their overall political position to the position they take on a specific racial policy—increasing government spending to fight black unemployment.

As figure 18 makes clear, in terms of general principles conservatives start out on the right and wind up on the right on racial issues, regardless of how they feel toward blacks. By contrast, liberals start out on the left, but where they wind up on racial issues depends very much on how they feel toward blacks. If liberals are racially tolerant, they strongly back government assistance for blacks; but if they are racially prejudiced, they break ranks and go over to the right. We are not suggesting that how conservatives feel toward blacks never makes any difference to positions they take on issues of race. On some issues, it makes a readily detectible difference. But it never makes a major one. Even where prejudice's impact is statistically significant, it is not politically significant. By contrast, racial prejudice makes a major difference to the positions that liberals take on specific racial issues. In short, on issues of race, the right tends to hold together; the left tends to splinter apart.

It would be one thing if this asymmetry between left and right applied only, or principally, to specially controversial issues of race. On an issue like affirmative action, it makes comparatively little difference if liberals divide their forces, since in any event the remainder of the public opposes it in overwhelming numbers. But as we have seen, liberals divide their forces over a whole array of issues dealing with race, among them government programs to promote employment for blacks, to provide a safety net for those in need of public assistance, and to fight discrimination in employment. These issues are very much part of the central terrain of American politics. They are, moreover, issues on which the distribution of political forces is at least roughly comparable. And just because they are issues on which liberals could prevail if they attracted to their side a segment of those on either the other side or the sidelines, it is all the more costly that, owing to the persisting impact of racial prejudice, they cannot hold on to nearly enough of their own forces.

CHAPTER FOUR

■

COLOR-BLIND POLITICS

Historically the civil rights movement took as its target aboli-
tion of the legally mandated inferiority of black Americans.
Fittingly, then, it took as its ideal a truly color-blind society where, as Martin Luther King Jr. prophesied, our children
would be judged "by the content of their character, not the
color of their skin." The success of the civil rights movement,
nearly everyone believed, marked the beginning of a historic
journey to racial equality. Ironically, it marked the foundering
of a historic public partnership between blacks and whites.

The partnership ran aground on several shoals, one of
which was formed by the call for black power and black separatism. Civil rights organizations, once dedicated to whites and
blacks working along side one another in a common cause,
expelled their white members as a matter of principle. Stokely
Carmichael, head of the Student Nonviolent Coordinating
Committee (SNCC), called for "killing honkies"; H. Rap Brown,
his successor, declared, "America won't come around, so we're
going to burn it down"; Malcolm X, speaking in behalf of the
extreme separatism of the Black Muslims under the leadership
of the honorable Elijah J. Mohammed, preached the "mystique
of blackness."[1]

As a form of symbolic politics, black separatism had a profound impact. Appeals to racial pride, racial nationalism, racial
solidarity took precedence. Integration as a moral idea was

eclipsed, and the very idea of common ground between blacks and whites was rejected as an expression of white hegemony. Assertions of black autonomy, coupled with demands for white reparations, replaced arguments addressed to the conscience of white Americans. Black power became a rallying cry, running from appeals to blacks to patronize black-owned businesses at one pole to a call for blacks to form their own nation at the other.

Judged by the test of improving the objective conditions of life for blacks, black separatism made no difference. But judged by the standard of transforming the climate of opinion, it made a profound difference—unfortunately for the worse. Failing to improve the lives of ordinary blacks, it succeeded in crippling the coalition most responsible for success in that very effort.

Black separatism is not the reason that America has a racial problem today. Its causes are a sticky compound of history and economics, made up of tenacious racial prejudice, the persistence of *de facto* racial segregation in housing and schooling, and the transformation of the American economy, including the withdrawal of semiskilled factory jobs from the inner cities. Though by no stretch the cause of the racial problem in America today, racial separatism has made it harder to relieve.

Increasingly, whites who had played a central role in the civil rights struggle distanced themselves from the politics of race, not because they doubted the urgency of achieving black progress but because they were troubled, or angered, by the new spirit of race separatism. Many of the most venomous battles over black power—for example, over "community control of schools" in Ocean Hill-Brownsville—are now largely forgotten. But the stream of race demagogues never dried up, with Al Sharpton and Louis Farrakhan succeeding Stokely Carmichael and Huey Newton. The institutionalization of preferential treatment—on the back of civil rights laws passed on the strength of a pledge to treat everyone, white or black, alike—created a sense of betrayal and anger as common on the left as on the right.

The ominous result: black and white Americans were driven even further apart. Working partnerships between blacks and whites did not disappear, but with civil rights laws on the books, a sympathetic Supreme Court to interpret them, and the Democratic party in control of Congress, it did not seem necessary to reach out and re-form an inclusive coalition for civil rights. American politics favors the status quo, and for a generation black political elites have been part of the political status quo.

Yet the objective conditions of life for many blacks have been getting steadily worse. The warning cry went out very nearly at the pinnacle of legislative success in the 1960s. America, the Kerner Commission declared, was threatening to split into two nations. One was white: educated, skilled, increasingly affluent, living under fair laws fairly administered. The other was black: embittered and alienated, victimized by poverty, crime, and social chaos, still caught in the coils of discrimination at the very moment they are proclaimed equal under the law.

It was a nightmare vision. Preventing it from coming to pass has been the understood premise of informed American thought about race and public policy for a generation. The responsibility of those heading American political, educational, and economic institutions was conceived as making sure that blacks have opportunities now, not a generation from now. And it was the need to see this assurance of opportunity honored, and not a commitment to an abstract doctrine of equality, that led so many among the politically aware and influential to back an array of public policies to overcome the racial divide, to bring black and white Americans together.

Whatever else these affirmative action policies have accomplished over the last quarter-century, it cannot be said that they have brought black and white Americans together. Ironically, the very urgency of the desire to reject the idea of America as two separate nations, black versus white, has persuaded many of the most thoughtful Americans of the necessity of racial separatism, at least temporarily. As Justice Blackman remarked in a now-famous formulation, "In order to get beyond racism, we must first take account of race."[2]

This premise of liberal thought on race was motivated by a manifestly benign intent, a desire to see blacks better off. Yet, as the *Federalist* papers argued long ago, democratic government can get into as much difficulty when it is in the hands of good men wishing to do good things as bad ones willing to do harm. Convinced of the goodness of their objectives, advocates of race-conscious policies found themselves inclined to view opposition as evidence of ill will. Far from being deterred by the inevitable clash of values—indeed, in part because they were aware that in any great enterprise a conflict of competing rights is unavoidable anyway—they swept forward.

But in a society where democratic citizenship matters, it is not enough for leaders to believe they are right, not enough even for them to be right. In the end, it is up to them to persuade the public as a whole that the goal they favor is worthy and that the means they make use of to accomplish it are fair. Persuading citizens that racial double standards are fair is undeniably what American political leadership has failed to do. It remains a conviction of the overwhelming number who make up American life that decisions about who should be hired, or who should be promoted, or who should be admitted to college or medical school should be done on the basis of the individual's merits, not ethnicity. Hence the largest part of their anger at racial double standards.

Advocates of a race-conscious politics dismiss, with impressive efficiency, this suggestion that America ought to aim at a color-blind politics. They charge that America is very far from color-blind. Turning a blind eye to the discrimination blacks still suffer and the disadvantages they still endure means turning the clock back. To proclaim that America must now be color-blind, with the job of assuring equal opportunity no more than half done, will guarantee that America becomes two nations, separate, hostile, and unequal.[3] Moreover, the argument runs, just so far as differences in outlook and practices between blacks and whites are part of the constitutive diversity of American society itself, it is in everyone's interest, white and black, that race-conscious policies work, for example, to ensure that no one getting a liberal arts education in the United States today can do so without seeing black faces or being exposed to black culture.

We are not unsympathetic to these concerns. But they must be judged by the evidence. As we have seen, race-conscious policies meet overwhelming opposition, with 8 or more out of every 10 whites disagreeing with preferential treatment for blacks, and at least 1 out of every 2 angry or upset over it. Moreover, as we have also seen, the anger of white Americans over race preferences is not provoked by a spasm of prejudice at the sight of black Americans at last being treated fairly. On the contrary, it reflects in the main a conviction that who gets ahead should be decided on the basis of individual merit and effort, as these ideas have been and continue to be understood by the largest number of citizens, liberal or conservative.

We have charted their resentment and sense of betrayal. But even in the face of their anger over the turn taken by the politics of race, and with all the opportunities that have been squandered, what we show in this chapter is that there is a far greater willingness to help those in need of help, including blacks, than has so far showed itself. Still more important, this support can be won for policies to help the worst-off, very much including the worst-off blacks.

Much depends on the quality of the case made for policies to help the worst-off. To win the most support, the strongest arguments need to be made. Arguments that blacks deserve assistance because of the historic injustices done to them have a public constituency. But arguments that appeal to universal moral intuitions that go beyond race have more power, not because they ignore the moral aspects of race as an issue in American life but because they are the very foundation of Americans' moral understanding of race. And just for this reason, policies to help the worst-off that now have the backing of only a minority can win the support of a majority, if we are willing to aim at a color-blind politics.

▪ ▪ ▪

Is it true that the very same policy framed in racially neutral terms gets markedly more public support than if it is formulated in racially specific ones? And, supposing the answer is yes, is the reason race prejudice?

In order to get the most comprehensive view possible, we have looked at public reactions to a number of different issues, among them enterprise zones, college scholarships, and school spending. And in order to get the most reliable view possible, we have made use of two independent surveys—the General Social Survey and the Race and Politics Study. For each issue, a randomly selected half of the sample was asked whether they agree or disagree with a policy framed in racial terms, while the other half was asked about the same policy framed in nonracial terms. For example, in the General Social Survey, one half of the respondents were asked whether they support or oppose giving business and industry special tax breaks "for locating in largely black areas," while the other half were asked whether they support or oppose giving business and industry special tax breaks "for locating in poor and high unemployment areas."[4]

Analogously, in the Race and Politics Study, one half of the respondents were asked if they would be willing to have their taxes raised a little "in order to improve educational opportunities for minorities," while the other half were asked if they would be willing to do so in order "to improve education in public schools." In all cases, then, we can assess the level of public support for government assistance specifically dedicated to blacks or on offer to anyone on the basis of need.

In these surveys, whites were markedly more likely to support a race-neutral policy than a race-specific one (figure 19). Moreover, the difference for whites was significant, not just in narrowly statistical terms but also in politically practical ones. Take spending more money on schools. When help was restricted to minorities, only a minority of whites (46 percent) were willing to see their taxes raised a little; however, when the extra money was going to improve things for all public school children, then a clear majority (65 percent) were willing to do so.

But doesn't this merely prove that a majority of whites favored a policy if they would benefit from it but opposed the very same policy if blacks benefit from it? Our findings are certainly consistent with the possibility that race prejudice was at work, but they are equally consistent with the possibility that policies advanced on universalistic grounds were more popular than those advanced on group-specific ones. What is needed is a direct test of both possibilities.

We call this test our School Tax Experiment. It starts with the premise that if prejudice really is the root factor undercutting support for strengthening educational opportunities for minorities (to take one example), then whites who dislike blacks should be more supportive of policies to help all school children than of those that concentrate on black school children; that is, the gap in levels of support among prejudiced whites should be large. Conversely, whites who like blacks should show less difference in their support of these two policies; their gap should be smaller.

In fact, the more positive white attitudes were toward blacks, the bigger, not the smaller, was the gap between sup-

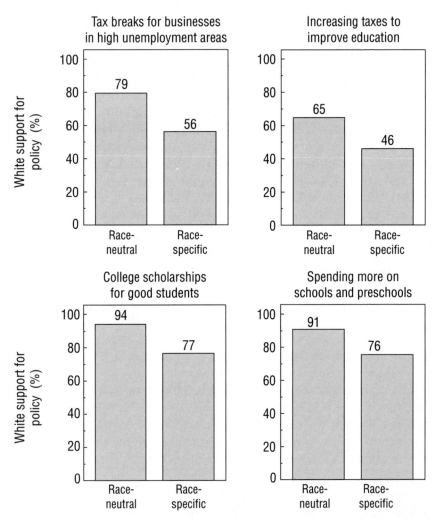

FIGURE 19
White Support for Race-Neutral versus Race-Specific Policies

Source: 1990 General Social Survey, 1991 Race and Politics Study. Number of respondents: tax breaks for businesses (GSS), from 544 to 557; tax for education (RAP), from 880 to 952; college scholarships (GSS), from 558 to 567; spending more on schools (GSS), from 555 to 563. Tests for statistical significance, race-neutral vs. race-specific: tax breaks to businesses, $t = 16.84$, $p < 0.001$; tax to improve education, $t = 7.96$, $p < 0.001$; college scholarships, $t = 13.80$, $p < 0.001$; spend more on schools, $t = 16.72$, $p < 0.001$.

port for race-neutral and race-specific policies: 80 percent of whites who were least prejudiced support race-neutral policies, whereas only 50 percent of them supported race-specific ones—a gap of 30 percentage points (figure 20).[5] Among the most prejudiced, on the other hand, the gap was much smaller. Clearly, whites who disliked blacks were much less likely to support policies to help all school children than were whites who like blacks—a finding that is consistent with the meanness of spirit characteristic of the prejudiced—and just because this meanness is general, not restricted to blacks, their racial prejudice cuts against supporting both versions of the policy,

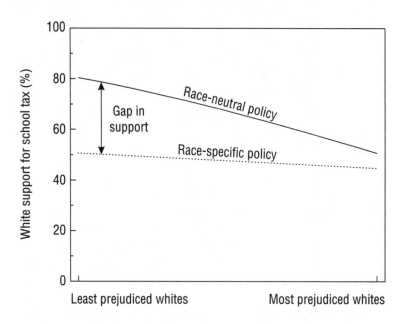

FIGURE 20
School Tax Experiment

Source: 1991 Race and Politics Study. Number of respondents ranges from 822 to 891. Tests of statistical significance: interaction of prejudice and policy, $p < 0.05$.

not just the race-centered one. Paradoxically, then, those who were racially tolerant, not those who were racially prejudiced, contributed disproportionately the winning advantage to policies that were formulated in racially neutral terms rather than racially specific ones.

Perhaps, then, whites are readier to support racially neutral policies rather than racially specific ones not because racially specific policies permit blacks to benefit but because they prohibit whites from doing the same. This is, for example, the suggestion of William Julius Wilson in his classic work, *The Truly Disadvantaged*, as well as in his follow-up book, *When Work Disappears*. According to this view, whites are reluctant to support race-centered policies because, though they too may need help from them, as whites they cannot get it. But if whites object to government assistance policies being targeted for blacks because they, as whites, cannot benefit, then whites who are most likely to benefit from such policies should be most likely to object. But however we measure material interest—whether in terms of family income, self-assessment of financial condition, or security of employment status—it plays no role of consequence in explaining why policies framed in racially inclusive terms are more popular than framed in racially restrictive ones (see table 6).

If it is not because of racism, nor because of self-interest, why are whites more likely to support a policy to help, for example, all school children (or all neighborhoods that are poor) than the same policy targeted at just black school children (or just black neighborhoods that are poor)?

A possible reason is this. Aiming at all who have a legitimate claim to assistance has more appeal than singling out for special treatment only one specific, limited group among them. According to this view, what limits the appeal of racially-targeted policies is not that they are targeted to benefiting blacks specifically but that they are restricted to benefiting a particular and limited group with a claim to assistance, at the

TABLE 6
White Support for Race-Neutral versus Race-Specific Policies to Aid School Children, by Self-Interest of Respondents

Measure of self-interest	White support for public schools (race-neutral)		White support for minorities (race-specific)	
Financial status[a]				
Improved	70%	(442)	50%	(421)
No change	59	(200)	46	(187)
Worse	62	(296)	42	(258)
Family income[b]				
Under $10,000	60%	(57)	42%	(53)
$10,000–$19,999	63	(120)	47	(108)
$20,000–$29,999	57	(156)	49	(135)
$30,000–$39,999	68	(154)	53	(144)
$40,000–$49,999	63	(126)	51	(127)
$50,000–$69,999	71	(154)	45	(137)
$70,000+	69	(132)	44	(120)
Employment status[c]				
Full time	66%	(556)	47%	(521)
Part time	68	(104)	56	(76)
Laid off	73	(14)	48	(6)
Unemployed	82	(23)	31	(18)
Retired	58	(126)	42	(139)
Disabled	47	(13)	36	(10)
Keeping house	52	(72)	45	(77)
Student	86	(27)	77	(17)

Source: 1991 Race and Politics Study.
[a] Interaction between type of tax and financial status: not significant.
[b] Interaction between type of tax and income: not significant.
[c] Interaction between type of tax and employment status: not significant.

cost of neglecting others with the same claim. If this is right, then policies aimed at an equivalently particularistic group of whites should be similarly limited in their appeal.

To see if this is indeed so, we conducted the Helping Hand Experiment. The key idea is to compare support for government assistance for blacks and for an equivalently particularistic group of whites. As an example of a specific and limited group of whites, we chose "new immigrants from Europe." Designating them "from Europe" allowed us to identify them as white without using the potentially off-putting word white. Describing them as "new immigrants" supplied a plausible basis for their needing government assistance. And characterizing them as "immigrants from Europe" distinguished them from immigrants that respondents perceive to be more threatening, either because they are not white or because they adhere to a different culture. But whether referred to as blacks or new immigrants from Europe, they were described as "people having problems with poverty." If the color of the skin of the person who gets help was crucial, then whites should be more willing to help fellow whites; however, if the decisive consideration was that a specific and limited group was being singled out for help, there should be no difference in how white Americans react to appeals to help blacks and those to help a group of fellow whites.

To see which alternative is right, in the Helping Hand Experiment a randomly selected half of the respondents were asked if they support government assistance for blacks; the other half, if they support government help for new immigrants from Europe. Strikingly, the race of the beneficiary did make a difference in whites' support for the policy, but in exactly the opposite direction than the presumption of white racism would suggest. Whites were significantly *more,* not less, willing to give a helping hand to blacks than to fellow whites; specifically, 84 percent support help for blacks, 76 percent support help for whites. There is, in short, reason to believe that whites are less likely to support a policy restricted to blacks than one extended to both blacks and whites, because it is group exclusive rather than group inclusive.

Of course, in deciding whether to support or oppose a particular proposal for government assistance, who gets help is only one consideration that citizens may take into account. How they are to be helped also matters.[6] Thus, whites are surely more likely to object if government assistance takes the form of welfare rather than, say, job training. Accordingly, the Helping Hand Experiment was designed to take into account not only who is to be helped but how they are to be helped. So in addition to, and independent of, experimentally varying whether whites or blacks were to be helped, half of the time government assistance took the form of "welfare" and half of the time "job training."

But arguments over government assistance are not just a matter of who is to be assisted or how they are to be assisted. They are also, we think fundamentally, arguments over why people should be helped. In the American popular culture there is a widely held idea that you ought to help people who have made an honest effort to help themselves but find themselves in need of help nonetheless. Accordingly, in a final complexity, half of the time those who were to be helped were described as "people who show they want to work out their own problems" and half of the time as "people who have trouble hanging on to jobs."

Both what kind of help was to be given, as well as what people may have done to deserve it, mattered (figure 21). More whites favored government assistance if it took the form of job training rather than welfare, and if those who were to be helped had tried to help themselves. Our real interest, however, was not in determining that either consideration mattered—we would have be astonished if they had not—but rather in establishing whether they counted the same for blacks as for whites. Specifically, in the eyes of whites, was the

FIGURE 21
Helping Hand Experiment

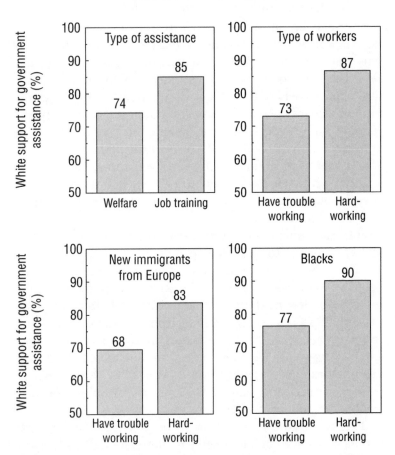

Source: 1991 Race and Politics Study. Number of respondents ranges from 388 to 1011. Tests of statistical significance: welfare vs. job training, $t = 5.66$, $p < 0.001$; trouble working vs. hard-working, $t = 7.04$, $p < 0.001$; new immigrants from Europe, trouble working/ hard-working, $t = 4.79$, $p < 0.001$; blacks, trouble working/hard-working, $t = 5.46$, $p < 0.001$.

charge that those who are relying on government help were feckless more stigmatizing applied to blacks than to whites?

Surely, common sense might lead us to suppose that stereotypes surrounding welfare have more sting attached to blacks than to whites. But this turned out to be one more case when common sense went awry. Judged in terms of support lost for government assistance, the charge that those who were getting help had not tried to help themselves cut just as deep applied to whites as to blacks. Viewed the other way around, a reason to cheer is that blacks were given the same credit for individual effort and accomplishment as whites.

Blacks got as much credit for trying to help themselves as whites, when all else was equal. The problem is that as a rule all else is not equal. When a group like blacks is perceived to benefit disproportionately from a program of government assistance *and* simultaneously is seen as not having tried to be self-reliant, there is a risk of being stigmatized. And as a moment's reflection will make plain, the risk is not small but large.

Think of the "welfare mess." At its inception the centerpiece program, Aid to Families with Dependent Children (AFDC), aimed to assist women who, most often on account of the death of their husband but in any event through no fault of their own, found themselves with the responsibility of raising small children alone but without enough money to do so. AFDC then had no racial character: it was about helping widows and small children, not blacks.

Much has changed since then. Seen through white eyes, welfare now has a black face. So, too, do crime and poverty. Blacks make up approximately 12 percent of the American population, or about 1 in every 8 Americans. In our study, a majority of whites believe that an absolute majority of the poor are black, and an even larger majority of whites believe that an absolute majority of those arrested for violent crimes last year were black. Statistically, these estimates are wildly off, which demonstrates only that ordinary Americans are not intuitive statisticians, not that they are unresponsive to reality. Race is a real problem in America partly because blacks are disproportionately likely to be poor, to be in need of AFDC, to be criminals, and to be victimized by criminals. It is this element of reality that drives the process of stigmatization.

Groups are at risk of being stigmatized if they come to be viewed as having been singled out, for a protracted period, for more than the ordinary measure of assistance. They are, moreover, at risk merely by virtue of being *perceived* to benefit disproportionately. The view of them as dependent on special assistance encourages a perception of them as undependable, lacking in initiative and self-reliance. Hence the danger of group stereotyping.

Just this danger is raised by the intersection of race and welfare in the minds of whites. Taking for granted that welfare is less popular than, say, job training, is it likely to be still less popular if its aim is to help blacks rather than whites? Translated into statistical terms, the question is whether the impact of describing government assistance as welfare is significantly larger when blacks are to benefit rather than whites. Our results are ambiguous. We can detect a tendency for welfare to be more unpopular when blacks rather than whites benefit, but strictly it is not statistically significant, hovering just over the conventional threshold.[7]

Given this suggestion that something is happening, if not quite what we had thought was going on, it is worth exploring the issue of stigmatization further. The race of the beneficiary of government assistance, taken by itself and in isolation from all other circumstances, may make no difference to whites, including those on the ideological right. But when all the elements of the "welfare mess"—help in the form of welfare, which redounds to the benefit of those who have not tried to help themselves and who are black besides—come together, things may change. Then race may become highly charged, especially for ideological conservatives. And this is just what happens. Even though conservatives respond quite negatively to the idea of welfare assistance for people who have proven themselves irresponsible, whether black or white, they respond still more negatively to blacks. By contrast, in the same circumstances liberals are more likely to favor government help for blacks than for white immigrants, so far as they respond differently to the two.[8] In short, the risk of racial stigmatization is real, not necessarily by the public as a whole but by the sizeable portion of it on the political right.

■ ■ ■

White objections to policies restricted to blacks, it is now commonly argued, are rooted not just in prejudice and self-interest but often in group interest.[9] According to this view, whites oppose race-targeted policies not for the moral reasons they cite— for example, in the name of a color-blind society— but because whites cannot benefit from them.

An idea may be right even if its political consequences are wrongheaded. The idea that the politics of race is fundamentally a matter of group interests, however, is both wrong and wrongheaded. Wrongheaded because, if the issue of race really were to reduce to group interests, given that blacks constitute only a small fraction of the citizenry, there never would have been a successful biracial effort in behalf of racial justice. Wrong because the coalition in pursuit of racial progress is potentially a political winner precisely because it is made up of both blacks and whites; indeed, in strictly numerical terms, made up principally of whites.

To be honest, we too fell into the trap we are now criticizing, underestimating the importance of moral arguments. What we realized, when we looked at the Helping Hand Experiment in retrospect, was the importance of whether the argument made in behalf of a policy designed to assist blacks itself went beyond race, invoking morally universalistic principles that apply regardless of race. In our surveys, to characterize the beneficiaries of a government policy as people who are in need and who have made an honest effort to deal with their problems on their own is to make a universalistic argument that they are deserving of help from others. It is universalistic because it applies across-the-board, rather than being specially invoked in behalf of one group at the expense of another. What the Helping Hand Experiment suggests, then, is that whites may be more willing to support race-specific policies if they are justified on universalistic, moral grounds.

Requiring blacks to drink from a water fountain marked "colored" was morally wrong. It would have been morally wrong whoever bore the brunt of it, whether black Americans, or Irish Americans, or Native Americans, or anyone else. What gave the civil rights movement its force was its insistence that discrimination on the basis of ethnicity violates our common humanity. Since the civil rights movement was at its peak, the range of moral arguments advanced in behalf of a more decent society has narrowed. The test of whether racial policies are good has increasingly come to center on whether blacks will be better off as a result of them. That is a very important consideration, but not the only one. Whether the means by which policies are to make blacks better off are fair also matters.

Speaking abstractly, no one would deny this. But consider the practice of artificially increasing the civil service test scores of blacks by an amount necessary to ensure that a satisfactory number of them are hired or promoted.[10] This practice of race norming, as it is called, turns the relation between ends and means on its head: since the end is desirable, namely, seeing that things are better for blacks, a once unimaginable means proves acceptable.

In a liberal democracy, so arbitrary a practice cannot retain its moral character, however desirable its moral objective. But it is not only the means that have come to be contested. Once the moral high ground of American public life, the politics of race has increasingly taken on the character of interest-group politics, because the values it serves have become increasingly particularistic. For example, much is made now of the value of ethnic diversity, with universities urged to select students and faculty and businesses to hire and promote employees on the basis of their ethnicity. From the point of view of a politics that is both democratic and liberal, the issue is not whether diversity is a desirable state of affairs, worth making an effort to achieve, nor even that it is only one of many values. The problem is that it is a particular kind of value.

It may be argued that whites will benefit, if as part of their liberal arts education they have an opportunity to know at first hand blacks and their culture. But as the best research of a generation ago demonstrated, contact only promotes tolerance if blacks and whites interact under conditions of equal status and as part of a common endeavor. As Gordon Allport remarked, "Only the type of contact that leads people to *do* things together is likely to result in changed attitudes. The principle is clearly illustrated in the multi-ethnic athletic team. Here the goal is all important; the ethnic composition of the team is irrelevant. It is the cooperative striving for the goal that engenders solidarity."[11] It cannot be said that present policies of preferential treatment strengthen the presumption of equal status; and whatever the effect of diversity policies might be were they differently administered, as presently implemented they are committed precisely to the proposition that ethnic composition *does* matter. It should not, in consequence, be surprising that the contemporary efforts launched on college campuses to promote tolerance have, according to the best research, had the very opposite effect, if they have had any, sharpening rather than erasing undergraduates' sense of invidious differences between ethnic groups.[12]

The political problem, then, is inescapable whether or not the legal issue is avoidable. Rewarding, and necessarily punishing, on the basis of diversity inescapably conflicts with the principle of equal treatment under the law as citizens understand it. A claim to equal treatment is pre-eminently a universalistic value; a claim to special treatment on the grounds of ethnicity is pre-eminently a particularistic value.

The problem is not that liberalism cannot offer good arguments in behalf of a particularistic value like ethnic diversity. The difficulty arises when diversity conflicts with a universalistic value like equal treatment under the law, as inevitably it does; then the arguments for particularistic benefits are not good enough. Hence the irony—and the accuracy—of liberalism's coming to be regarded as a philosophy of special interests. Liberalism's advocacy of ethnic diversity is rooted in principle, even in the face of its own political self-interest. But its very awareness that it is faithful to principle, sometimes to its own disadvantage, has blinded it to the fact that it has pledged itself to a principle that is—and in the end ought to be—subordinate to universalistic principles.

Although not all liberals reject an appeal for color-blind politics, nearly all who do reject it are liberals. In their judgment, to insist that our politics conform to a color-blind standard is to ensure that it will be color-discriminatory. Some argue that race-conscious policies remain necessary on the grounds that race prejudice and discrimination remain a force: as Cornel West declares, "Given the history of this country, it is a virtual certainty that without affirmative action racial and sexual discrimination would return with a vengeance."[13]

Viewed objectively, to prophesy the return of racial and sexual discrimination "with a vengeance" is to take leave of the evidence. But it is important not to be distracted by polemical arguments and wind up neglecting better ones on which a critique of a color-blind politics can be grounded. The issue is not whether, if American politics were to aim at being color-blind, blacks will be treated worse than whites. It may be enough that they will then fare less well than now. After all, details of specific admission, hiring, and promotion schemes aside, the point of the structure of administrative regulations and judicial rulings now in place is to increase the probability that explicit and ample consideration be given to the needs and circumstances of blacks. If blacks lose their special status, if they become just one group among many in the kaleidoscope of American pluralism, is it unreasonable to fear that they will be lost in the shuffle?

We respect the reasons for this concern, but we want nevertheless to suggest that if our politics committed itself to being color-blind, it would be to the advantage, not the disadvantage, of those blacks most in need of assistance.

Politics, from the perspective of citizens, is not so much about who gets what as it is about, more fundamentally, who *should* get what. The argument over race in public policy cannot be understood without realizing that, in the eyes of citizens, it is a moral argument. What counts, for them, is not simply who is to benefit from government assistance. As important is why they should benefit.[14] The two are not the same, and if we are to see how possibly to move forward in the politics of race, they need to be kept straight.

Consider government assistance, say, in the form of job training. For argument's sake, suppose we are specifically interested in a policy to serve blacks and other minorities. Obviously, it is possible to urge its adoption on the grounds that blacks have historically been ill-treated, and given the continuing legacy of prejudice and discrimination they have suffered, it is appropriate that those among them who are out of work and who lack the skills to get a job receive some help in preparing themselves for employment. Indeed, this has become, for a generation now, the principal line of argument in behalf of social welfare policies to assist blacks.

Yet, exactly the same objective (to help blacks) through exactly the same means (by job training) can be advanced on grounds that are not restricted to or even centered on considerations of race. It is perfectly possible to argue that such programs of assistance merit support because those who are out of work and need to learn new skills to get a job and stand on their own feet deserve a helping hand, regardless of race. The same program can thus be argued for on two different grounds: that blacks ought to receive its assistance given the price they have uniquely paid for being black or, more universalistically, that people who are in need of this kind of assistance should have a chance to benefit from it, and they should be able to do so independently of whether they happen to be black.

We believe the current impasse over race can be broken, and to see how possibly to accomplish this, it is crucial to compare and contrast the power of these two different lines of argument, one confined to considerations of race and one that reaches beyond it. Hence the Regardless of Race Experiment.[15] The experiment examines public support for job training programs. Of the various reasons why the willingness to support programs like this matters, perhaps the most important is this. Affirmative action, although it has the glamour of controversy, does not touch the lives of those who are worst off. By contrast, job training programs, among other social welfare programs, are part of an effort to help those most in need of help.

In the Regardless of Race Experiment, the justification for government assistance was varied. One half of the time, it was justified on the grounds that blacks have historically been mistreated; the other half, it was justified on grounds regardless of race, but always, whether the argument was confined to race or reached beyond it, blacks were to benefit. The purpose of the experiment was thus to see if public support for job training programs can be increased if the argument for government assistance goes beyond race even though the policy is nonetheless restricted to blacks. Accordingly, a randomly selected half of the sample was asked:

> As you may know, unemployment among blacks is high. Some
> people believe that the government in Washington should be

responsible for providing job training to them *because of the historic injustices blacks have suffered.*[16] Other people believe that the government is basically doing as much as it can and that it is now up to blacks to take care of their own problems. If you had to choose, would you say it is mostly the responsibility of the government to provide job training for blacks, or is it is mostly up to blacks to take care of their own problems?

Arguments, it is clear, were being made both for and against the program, but the central element in both was race.

By contrast, the remaining half of the sample was asked:

As you may know, unemployment among blacks is high. Some people believe that the government in Washington should be responsible for providing job training to them, not because they are black, but *because the government ought to help people who are out of work and want to find a job, whether they're white or black.*[17] Other people believe that the government is basically doing as much as it can and that it is now up to people, white or black, to take care of their own problems. If you had to choose, would you say it is mostly the responsibility of the government to provide job training for blacks, or is it mostly up to blacks to take care of their own problems?

The political terms of reference remained exactly the same— job training programs run by the government in Washington, and the recipients of the benefits were clearly identified as black—but in the second case the arguments both pro and con were explicitly made regardless of race .

What difference did it make whether arguments for a policy stuck to race or reached beyond it? Whites were approximately half again as likely to support job training programs for blacks if the policy argument, rather than being confined to narrowly racial grounds, was made on grounds that were universal, applying equally to blacks and whites. Specifically, whereas 21 percent of whites supported job training when the appeal was racial, 34 percent supported it when the appeal was universal.

To observe that a policy to help blacks wins the support of

more whites if it is advanced on color-blind principles is not to say that it is guaranteed to win the backing of a majority of them. Certainly, in this instance it did not. Nor should this be surprising. As we pointed out, programs that restrict government assistance to blacks handcuff their appeal to the public as a whole, and not because of racism. Moreover, even though arguments that reach beyond race are more effective than those restricted to it, it does not follow that a majority can be conjured up for a race-targeted program at will. Social welfare policies, like job training, are part of the deep cleavage over the proper role of government in America: they were contested before the issue of race moved to the center of public attention, and to a moral certainty will remain contested when it recedes from attention.

Whether or not a supportive majority is guaranteed, the lesson of the Regardless of Race Experiment should be clear. It is better to make use of arguments that reach beyond race—to contend that help should be given because people are in need of it and can benefit from it, regardless of their race. Better for whom? Better for blacks. The cloud of cynicism blanketing the idea that our politics should be color-blind notwithstanding, precisely the point of the experiment is that even if policies target government assistance to blacks, it is still better to argue on grounds that reach beyond race.

But there is another consideration at least as important as the level of support for programs argued on color-blind principles. What matters politically is not only how many can be won over by arguments that go beyond race, but who they are. To begin with, support is hugely boosted among liberals, the crucial core constituency for social welfare programs, by concentrating on color-blind principles (figure 22, top). Only 40 percent of liberals support job training if the argument for the policy is restricted to considerations of race; but if it reaches beyond race, 55 percent support it. Conservatives, by contrast, cannot be rallied in support of programs like job training on

FIGURE 22
Regardless of Race Experiment

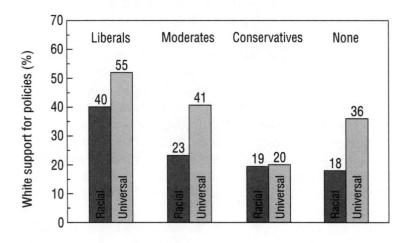

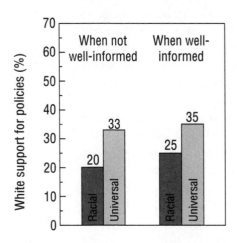

Source: 1994 Multiple Investigator Study. Number of respondents ranges from 599 to 649.

whatever ground they are advocated, whether race-specific or race-neutral.

From a liberal perspective, the choice whether or not to support a job training program seems to reduce to whether or not one has the compassion and the willingness to sacrifice for others who are less fortunate. Just because the choice, so viewed, seems a matter of humanitarian values rather than political judgment, it is difficult for liberals to appreciate the sincerity of conservatives. So it regularly seems to the left that the resistance of the right must somehow be grounded in considerations of race, and that its objection to government assistance for blacks can be overcome, if indeed it can be overcome, by shaming them into conceding that it is the right thing to do notwithstanding the fact that blacks are to benefit from it.

But this misses entirely the merits viewed from the right, and by underestimating the sincerity of the conservative objection, underestimates its constancy. From a conservative perspective, Washington-run job training programs, however well-intentioned, risk doing more good than harm, and not only to the larger society but also to the very people they are ostensibly supposed to benefit. And just because the objection from the right is political rather than racial, it cannot be got round by reaching beyond race.

Ironically, then, the advantage of moving race politics onto a color-blind plane is not that it provides a way to escape politics, by shifting the argument over policies to a plane where only moral considerations count, but rather that it provides a way to benefit from it. On the one side, if the argument for job training is made on the basis of values that are color-blind, support from the largest part of the public, which regards itself as free of ideological commitments, doubles (figure 22, top). On the other side, so too does support from that part of the public which regards itself as liberal. It thus pays twice over to argue on moral common ground.

The public's response to public policy, these findings drive home, can vary to a degree that matters politically, depending on political argument itself. The lesson of the Regardless of Race Experiment, so viewed, is this. The strongest arguments in behalf of programs to deal with issues of race need not be confined to considerations of race. Indeed, the most effective way to increase the coalition in support of policies that directly improve the lives of the worst-off blacks is to reach beyond race itself and appeal to moral common ground—to principles that apply regardless of race.

It would be one thing if arguing on moral common ground was more effective only because it influenced most those most susceptible to influence—namely, the least well-informed. In politics, persuasion of this form tends to represent a pyrrhic victory. Pyrrhic because, insofar as those most likely to be swayed are those who are the least well-informed, the boost in support will be confined to those least likely to act on it politically. However, our data show that the appeal of a universal argument is just as effective among those whose political understanding is high as it is among those whose grasp of politics is weaker (figure 22, bottom).[18] For those concerned about the efficacy of a color-blind politics, this is a finding that matters. Since the most informed are as responsive as the least, there is reason to believe that *what* is being argued makes a difference.

The Regardless of Race Experiment explores the politics of government assistance targeted by race but justified on grounds that reach beyond race. What we examine next is the politics of policies that are color-blind with respect both to who is to be helped and why they should be helped.

■ ■ ■

In the last quarter of a century, both present circumstances and future prospects have dramatically improved for middle-class blacks; in contrast, the objective conditions of life for less well-off blacks have deteriorated.[19] It is argued that the needs of better-off blacks should nonetheless remain at the center of public attention, since they are not yet as well-off as well-off whites.[20] We shall, however, proceed on the assumption that whether or not programs that primarily assist better-off blacks should be retained in place or not, primacy of attention now ought to go to the needs of those who are badly off, including those who are both black and badly off. Accordingly, we want to explore how much public support for social welfare policies can be boosted by making them color-blind through and through—that is, by ensuring that they aim at all in need, not just those who are black, *and* by making the case for assistance on the basis of a moral principle that goes beyond race, not just on the basis of appeals restricted to considerations of race.

The Color-Blind Experiment was conducted to assess the calculus of public support for color-blind government assistance. One out of three people, randomly selected, was asked:

> Some people believe that the government in Washington should be responsible for improving the social and economic condition of blacks who are born into poverty. They say that because of the continuing legacy of slavery and discrimination we have a special obligation to help blacks to get ahead. Other people believe that the strength of the American way of life is that people should deal with their problems on their own. If you had to choose, would you say the government should take responsibility for improving the social and economic conditions of blacks who are born into poverty, or should the government stay out of it?

In the first condition, then, the policy was targeted and justified on racial lines. In the second condition, the argument remained the same in every respect but one. The interviewer said:

> Some people believe that the government in Washington should be responsible for improving the social and economic

condition of blacks who are born into poverty. They say that we ought to try to make sure that everyone has an equal opportunity to succeed. Other people believe that the strength of the American way of life is that people should deal with their problems on their own. If you had to choose, would you say the government should take responsibility for improving the social and economic conditions of blacks who are born into poverty, or should the government stay out of it?

In the final condition, the beneficiaries of the program were broadened, to include all people born into poverty, not just blacks specially, *and* the justification for assistance was made on the universalistic grounds of equal opportunity, not one confined to issues of racial justice. Specifically, the issue was framed as follows:

Some people believe that the government in Washington should be responsible for improving the social and economic conditions of people who are born into poverty. They say that we ought to try to make sure that everyone has an equal opportunity to succeed. Other people believe that the strength of the American way of life is that people should deal with their problems on their own. If you had to choose, would you say the government should take responsibility for improving the social and economic conditions of people who are born into poverty, or should the government stay out of it?

Is there a politically significant gain in pursuing a color-blind politics? The answer, based on our data, is unequivocally yes (figure 23, top). When the obligation to achieve equal opportunity was cast in narrowly racial terms—when, that is, it was confined to assisting blacks and justified on the narrow ground of making up for the continuing legacy of slavery and discrimination—only 31 percent of whites agreed that the "federal government in Washington should be responsible for improving the social and economic conditions of blacks." When the program was confined to helping blacks but was justified not on racially specific but on morally universalistic grounds, then support for it went up significantly, to 42 per-

FIGURE 23
Color-Blind Experiment

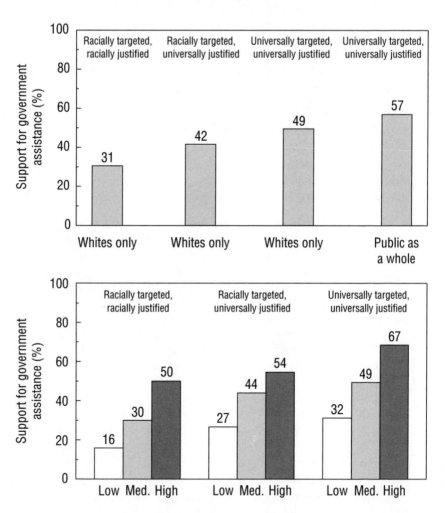

Source: 1994 Multiple Investigator Study. Number of respondents ranges from 399 to 415.

cent. But when assistance for those born into poverty was presented on genuinely color-blind terms, with neither its beneficiaries nor its justification restricted by race, one in every two whites backed it. Of course, in gauging the strength of a political coalition, we need to take into account the public as a whole, minority as well as nonminority. Looking at citizens as a whole, when the issue of inequality is posed in universal terms and argued for on universal grounds, a decisive majority—57 percent—believe that government should take responsibility for improving the social and economic conditions of those born into poverty.

We are not suggesting that the politics of public policy is merely a matter of marketing. It is a matter of argument. The public's reaction to public policy hinges in part on what is proposed by way of public action, and on what arguments are made both for and against what is being proposed. For politics is very much a matter of argument and counterargument. What the experiment demonstrates is the strength of a color-blind appeal to the value of equal opportunity, not in isolation from other values but in head-to-head competition with the value of self-reliance. Our respondents had a real choice, with a potent value evoked in behalf of opposition to government assistance as well as in support of it. The fact that a majority could nonetheless be won for a truly color-blind politics thus offers a reminder of a lesson most of us once knew but, perhaps because it was so simple, many of us have forgotten. An appeal to equality of opportunity gains strength if it is made on behalf of all equally, and not on behalf of some selectively.

But why can whites more readily be persuaded to support policies that go beyond race? Surely, one possibility is that whites are willing to join and back a policy to help those born into poverty, on color-blind terms, precisely because it is *not* put in terms of helping blacks. On this view, color-blind politics are popular not because they reach out to a wider ideal but because they put out of sight the divisive ideal of racial justice.

In order to assess whether this view is correct or not, we attempted to gauge how committed whites are to the value of racial equality by taking account, simultaneously, of their views on a number of matters, among them the strength with which they reject a suggestion that we should give up the goal of racial equality "because blacks and whites are so very different"; whether they believe it is more important to promote traditional religious values in politics and society or to promote racial harmony and equality between blacks and whites; and, finally, whether they think it is more important to maintain pride and respect for our country or to promote racial harmony and equality between blacks and whites. If it is true that a color-blind politics owes its strength to its appeal to those unsympathetic to the value of racial equality, or even to those merely indifferent to it, then the impact of the variations in the Color-Blind Experiment should be strongest for them. But what we found is that this is not true at all. Putting policy on a morally universalistic basis has as strong an appeal for those for whom the value of racial equality itself had the strongest appeal (figure 23, bottom).

On the assumption that social welfare programs can effectively help those most in need of help, then a way forward is possible. Public support for these programs can be markedly boosted by making the argument for them on the basis of moral principles that cut across race; or by establishing that the objective of these programs is to help those in need of help, regardless of race; or both. Either approach gains adherents both among whites who are indifferent to the needs of blacks and those who are genuinely concerned about them. And if these policies are color-blind with respect to both who should be helped and why, instead of enjoying the support of only a minority, they can win the backing of a majority.

■　■　■

One premise of a color-blind politics is that blacks and whites can join together in support of policies to assist those who are badly off, whether black or white, because they themselves share common ground not excluding issues of race. It is now more often presumed that when blacks and whites look at race, they see two different realities, and in the light of the sensational stories that make headlines, this may seem self-evidently so. But although we are far from denying the genuine differences between black and white Americans, we believe it is worth the effort to see if there is also common ground.

We want to begin by underlining the differences between them, specifically with respect to the question of responsibility. As a first and very rough representation of the views of both blacks and whites as to why blacks remain worse off than whites, we asked both to assess blame: Is it whites, in their view, who are mostly to blame, or is it blacks, or do both share the blame equally? Clearly, blacks and whites did not have the same view of the matter (figure 24). Whites were twice as likely as blacks to believe that blacks are mostly to blame. To be sure, only a small fraction of either whites or blacks felt that blacks are mostly to blame; by contrast, far and away the largest number—two thirds in the case of whites, more than three-quarters in the case of blacks—felt that blacks and whites are equally to blame.

But, then, an invitation to suggest that both are to blame may have a superficial attraction of appearing evenhanded, and so, in an effort to understand more exactly what it might mean to say this, we pushed on to investigate further the issue of blame and responsibility. Specifically, we asked those who thought that whites were at least partly to blame if they thought whites intentionally wished blacks to be worse off. That is, do whites really try to keep blacks down, or do they do it without meaning to? On this question blacks and whites differed markedly. One in every two blacks (53 percent) said that whites try to keep blacks down on purpose, whereas only one out of every four whites (28 percent) said that whites keep blacks down intentionally.

Having underlined that there are indeed differences, we

FIGURE 24
Who Is to Blame for the Condition of Blacks,
by Race of the Respondent

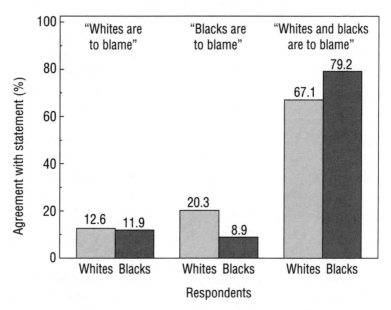

Source: 1991 Race and Politics Study. Number of respondents ranges from 236 to 1,620.

believe that the best way to see if there is common ground is to allow blacks and whites the freedom to discuss the problem of race in their own words. So instead of requiring them to choose between alternatives that we defined for them, we instead invited them to define the problem of racial inequality in terms they themselves chose, remarking to everyone that "Statistics show that the average black person in America is worse off than the average white person," and then asking them, "What do you suppose caused this difference?"

In analyzing their answers, which were taken down as near

to verbatim as possible, we categorized the reasons they gave for blacks being worse off than whites as finely as possible, and then, so that the detail of their answers should not obscure their overall thrust, categorized their specific responses in larger, summary groupings. These summary groupings we organized under three headings: explanations that center on factors external to blacks, those that center on factors internal to them, and those that are tied up with their immediate circumstances.

Our objective was to ensure that respondents were free to define the problem of racial inequality in their own terms, instead of having to fit the round pegs of their ideas into the square holes of our point of view. Everyone was therefore free to mention as many different factors, of as many different kinds, as they wished.

Looking at the specific explanations that blacks and whites gave when they were free to talk in their own words about why blacks are worse off than whites, we were struck by the similarity in their views (figure 25). Blacks and whites were nearly equally likely to explain blacks being worse off than whites in terms of factors over which blacks have no control—among them, inadequate schools, and a lack of funding for education.

To say that their responses were similar is not to say that they were identical. Blacks, for example, were more likely than whites to point to a lack of economic—as distinct from a lack of educational—opportunity, while whites were more likely than blacks to attribute blacks being worse off to characteristics of blacks themselves, and in particular to a lack of effort and motivation on the part of blacks. Whites were also more likely to point to the circumstances in which blacks find themselves, and in particular, to problems within the black family. These differences, however, were a matter of degree. For example, just over 1 in every 5 whites cited problems in the black family as part of the reason blacks remain worse off than whites; but then again, just over 1 in every 6 blacks said the same thing.

FIGURE 25
Why Blacks Are Worse Off than Whites,
by Race of the Respondent

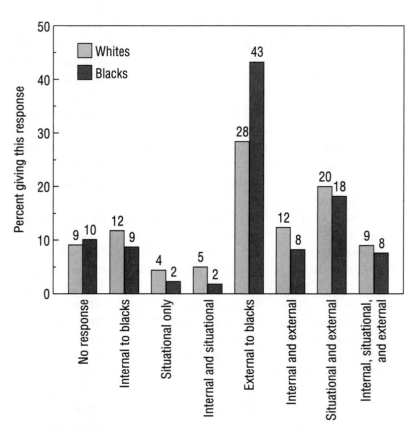

Source: 1991 Race and Politics Study. Number of respondents ranges
from 248 to 1,748.

Moreover, if blacks often point to discrimination on the part of whites as part of the problem, whites are just as likely to do the same.

Recognizing the differences in emphasis, we were struck by the relative absence of racial polarization, the more so as our respondents were free to define the problem of racial inequality in their own terms, rather than having to confront it on ours. It was emphatically not the case that blacks saw one reality of race, and whites another, with blacks fixing the blame for blacks being worse off on whites and whites pointing the finger at blacks. On the contrary, most cited the same factors, and to approximately the same degree. So far as they differed, the principal point of difference was the extent to which blacks, if they pointed to external factors, did so exclusively, while whites more often saw a mix of factors, external and internal, as well. What was striking is the amount of common ground between blacks and whites.

This impression of common ground is virtually absent from public discussion of race as an issue in American life. There is now a virtually unchallenged presumption that, looking at the issue of race, blacks and whites see altogether different realities. Certainly, this is what we expected to see—that was, after all, why we wanted them to be free to express their own point of view in their own words. But it was the similarity of blacks and whites' views, not the dissimilarity, that stood out. We want, therefore, to take seriously the possibility that whites and blacks in America share more in common than is commonly appreciated: and just because we ourselves wish to believe that they do, we have devised a specially demanding test to establish whether they do or not.

To say that a group of people—blacks, for example—should work their way up has become suspect. An insistence on self-reliance, it is now widely suspected, has become a symbolic cloak used by whites who dislike blacks to cover their prejudice politely. The underlying premise is that whites are applying to blacks a standard of conduct they would not apply to fellow whites. This premise is worth critical examination because, as we shall show, the current overreadiness to make accusations of prejudice can distort values that whites and blacks hold in common.

Thus our No Special Favors Experiment. One half of all respondents (randomly selected) were asked if they agree or disagree (and whether they do so strongly or somewhat) with the following statement:

> In the past, the Irish, the Italians, the Jews and many other minorities overcame prejudice and worked their way up. Blacks should do the same without any special favors.

The other half of the respondents were asked not about blacks but about "new immigrants from Europe"—a designation deliberately chosen to make plain that the people being referred to are white without explicitly saying so and putting people on their guard. In short, one half of whites and one half of blacks interviewed were asked whether blacks should work their way up, the other half whether new immigrants from Europe should make their own way.

White respondents said overwhelmingly that blacks should work their way up, just as Italians and others had done, without any special favors (figure 26). But whites were equally likely to believe that "new immigrants from Europe" should also make their own way up, without any special favors. In short, to assert that whites expose themselves as racists when they declare that black Americans ought to work their way up "without any special favors" is false.

Now, consider the reactions of blacks. Cynicism about the commitment of Americans to a color-blind standard has increasingly itself become color-blind: if there is little faith that whites, free to choose between whites and blacks, will not favor whites, there is no stronger faith that blacks, free to choose between blacks and whites, will not favor blacks. But

FIGURE 26
No Special Favors Experiment

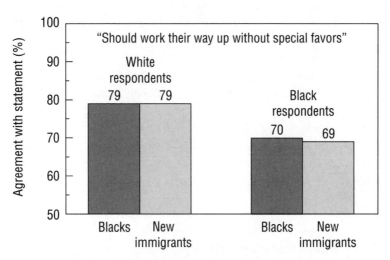

Source: 1991 Race and Politics Study. Number of respondents ranges from 105 to 886. Tests of statistical significance: for whites, blacks vs. New immigrants, n.s.; for blacks, blacks vs. new immigrants, n.s.

cynicism about blacks has been fueled not by systematic evidence on how ordinary blacks make up their mind—since the overriding fact is the dearth of information on what ordinary blacks think—but by highly publicized stories of individual black political figures who have exhibited the failings characteristic of demagogues whatever their color. Knowing little directly about ordinary blacks, even otherwise knowledgeable whites have entertained the idea that when considerations of race are relevant, blacks would take a position primarily with an eye on whether it was advantageous to blacks.

Just because of this cynicism, two aspects of the No Special Favors Experiment are worth underlining. First, blacks, like whites, are overwhelmingly likely to believe that others—new

immigrants from Europe, in this instance—ought to take responsibility for working their way up, without any special
favors (figure 26). Second, and no less important, blacks were
just as likely to believe that blacks should take responsibility
for working their way up, without any special favors, as they
were to believe that whites should do so (figure 26). In short,
black Americans also support the ethic of self-reliance, and in
a way that is altogether principled. Blacks were as willing to
apply to themselves the requirements of independence and
individual effort that they applied to others. For better and for
worse, and to an extent which deserves to be appreciated
again, black Americans and white Americans share the same
culture.

■   ■   ■

A biracial coalition made progress possible in the past, and
there will not be new policies put in place to help those who
are badly off, whether black or white, unless blacks and whites
again make common cause. What our results demonstrate is
that policies to assist those who are badly off, even if they
initially enjoy the support of only a minority, can attract the
support of a majority provided they aim to assist those who
need assistance whether black or white, and are advanced on
grounds that apply regardless of race. It is by appealing to the
values that black and white Americans hold in common that
they will act in common.

To say that a commitment to a color-blind politics is worth
undertaking is to call for a politics centered on the needs of
those most in need. It is not to argue for a politics in which
race is irrelevant, but in favor of one in which race is relevant
so far as it is a gauge of need. Above all, it is to call for a politics
which, because it is organized around moral principles that
apply regardless of race, can be brought to bear with special
force on the issue of race.

It will still be objected that a color-blind politics is only possible in a color-blind society. That gets the relationship between ideals and reality exactly the wrong way around. As Henry Bauer has remarked, "Those who hold ideals, no matter that they are unattainable, are likely to behave more in accord with them than will people who do not hold those ideals."[21] We shall approach the reality of a color-blind society just so far as we commit ourselves to the ideal of one.

CHAPTER FIVE

■

LIBERALISM'S PREDICAMENT

It is liberalism's lasting honor to have been in the vanguard of a crusade to achieve racial equality in America. Liberalism has by no means been the only force at work, nor always the most important, particularly in the early years when black leaders and black communities, acting on their own initiative and drawing on their own resources, launched the modern civil rights movement. But absent liberalism's commitment, the revolution in the legal and political standing of American blacks since the midcentury would have been inconceivable.

The historic changes in the 1950s and 60s notwithstanding, the struggle for racial equality has been floundering for some time. Black Americans have made historic advances, but the racial disparities that persist in unemployment, out-of-wedlock births, poverty, imprisonment, criminal victimization, infant mortality, and life expectancy are undeniable. To some, the reasons that the movement for civil rights and racial equality has stalled are obvious. Viewed from the left, the problem is both that not enough has been done, the rhetoric of a "war" on poverty notwithstanding, and that much of what was once done has been undone by the right, capitalizing on the prejudices and fears of white Americans.[1] Viewed from the right, the morass of poverty, illegitimacy, and crime in which so many blacks are mired was created, or at any rate aggravated, by what was done by the social welfare policies of the left, particularly through expansion of welfare and government assistance and lowering of standards of individual responsibility.[2] And viewed from either side, blacks are surely worse off because of changes in the American economy, most notably the loss of low-skill, good-wage jobs in the inner city.[3] Blacks are, moreover, worse off than other ethnic minorities because these changes in the economy have been coupled with the persistence of residential segregation, which imprisons so many blacks in inner cities, cutting them off from good schools, job opportunities, and safe neighborhoods in which to live and raise their families.[4]

The issue that we want to address here is not why the crusade to achieve racial equality has stalled but what can be done to reawaken support for it. Our premise is this: if there is to be a second crusade, liberals will have to play a principal role. Partly because of past experience, still more because of principle, conservatives are not in a position to dedicate themselves to a collective effort to ameliorate racial inequality. The movement for equality has come to be at the heart of the liberal conviction, and without liberalism's continuing commitment to it, the movement will come to an exhausted and bitter end.

But liberalism cannot just carry on as it has. It has not launched a new, large-scale initiative on the issue of race in a decade, investing its energies instead in defensive battles to hang on to the gains of the 1960s and 70s, battles it is now losing. Nor is it merely the struggle against racial inequality which has faltered. Liberalism itself is in trouble, and not only over race, even if that is its most visible ground of dissension. It has become vulnerable, now as never before, to a moral as well as a pragmatic critique.

The questioning of liberalism is being conducted on a number of fronts. It has been subjected, most obviously and successfully, to a critique organized around conservative principles, and it has additionally had to bear the anger of those resentful of its efforts in behalf of black Americans. But independent of those attacks, criticism has developed from a quite different direction. By virtue of the terms of its commitment to racial equality—above all, in consequence of its advocacy of affirmative action—liberalism has opened itself up to challenge on the basis of liberal principles themselves. From the perspective of a racial liberal, the politics of affirmative action are clear, not in exact detail but in broad outline. Certainly, liberals have no doubt about the policy's unpopularity. But they also generally agree about the principal reasons for its unpopularity. These include the persistence of white racism, however vigorously denied or artfully disguised; the reluctance of many whites, even setting racial prejudice aside, to make real sacrifices to achieve racial equality, when push comes to shove; the resentment that so many whites harbor at the special treatment they believe blacks receive; the anxiety and frustration that many now experience as their own hopes for jobs and advancement wither in a stagnant economy.

According to the standard view, the liberal predicament over affirmative action arises because the left has been unable to persuade the center or the right of the merits of its case. In fact, this standard view greatly underestimates liberalism's predicament. As our List Experiment demonstrated, when liberals believe that they can express their feelings about race-conscious policies without anyone being able to tell how they feel, they turn out to be as angry about affirmative action as conservatives. Those on the political left—both people who describe themselves as liberals and those who describe themselves as Democrats—are deeply split over affirmative action, indeed, divided more or less up the middle. Liberalism's predicament does not arise from its failure to make its case for the necessity of a race-conscious agenda to the public as a whole. Its real predicament is rooted in its failure to persuade itself.

■ ■ ■

It has become standard among liberals to charge that opposition to affirmative action, if not always inspired by racism, is at any rate bolstered by it; or that if out-and-out racism does not lie behind opposition to affirmative action, then anxiety over future job prospects is at work; or if individual self-interest is not at work, then "collective" self-interest is responsible, with whites acting to promote the interests of whites as a whole. All of these charges suggest that the challenge to affirmative action, however it may be dressed up on public occasions, does not really represent a principled objection to a particular public policy but rather a form of prejudice or self-interest.

There is no doubt that some whites oppose affirmative action out of prejudice. The question, however, is whether racial prejudice is a major factor promoting opposition to affirmative action or a minor one. Whites who dislike blacks overwhelmingly dislike affirmative action—this comes as no surprise. What commands attention is that whites who *like* blacks oppose it, too, and very nearly as overwhelmingly. Looking at only the 25 percent of the public whose attitudes toward blacks is most favorable, we discovered that opposition to affirmative action in this group is overwhelming, with between 7 and 8 out of every 10 objecting to it. It is simply wrong to suppose that racial prejudice is a primary source of opposition to affirmative action.

Racism turns out to be just one of a string of explanations offered for opposition to affirmative action that don't cash out. For example, contrary to the suggestion that opposition to the race-conscious agenda is being driven by apprehension over economic futures, the level of opposition has been as pronounced in economic good times as in bad. Contrary to the suggestion that opposition to affirmative action is rooted in the spirit of individualism and the ethic of self-reliance characteristic of American capitalism, the policy is comparably unpopular when deployed in behalf of groups other than blacks in countries other than the United States. Contrary to the suggestion that the contemporary furor over affirmative action represents the response of "angry white males" who perceive themselves to be paying the price, younger men are less, not more, likely than older men to oppose it, and women are overwhelmingly opposed to it as well. Opposition to affirmative action is one-sided, intense, and remarkably invariant over time.

What is truly driving the debate over affirmative action and what does the clash over it say about the character of American culture? Our findings indicate that the most fundamental factor behind opposition to affirmative action is one of principle. In its original meaning, affirmative action called for an extra effort to be made to ensure fair consideration for black candidates for job or college admission; the proof of fairness was the fairness of the selection process. Affirmative action has subsequently come to mean ensuring selection of black or minority candidates; now proof of fairness is the selection of an agreed upon number of black candidates.

As our Two Meanings Experiment showed, about 2 out of every 3 white Americans believe that "an extra effort should be made to make sure that qualified blacks are considered for university admission," and did so in the face of being expressly told that some people feel that making an extra effort in behalf of blacks has the effect of discriminating against whites. It is, in short, not true that whites are unwilling to reach out across the racial divide. In fact, a clear majority of whites believe that an extra effort *should* be made to ensure blacks are judged on their merits, and not on the color of their skin.

It is against this commitment to ensuring fair treatment that the anger and resentment generated by preferential treatment needs to be set. The largest number of citizens find it unacceptable that a person who is less qualified on academic criteria be admitted to a college, because he is black, in preference to a person who is more academically qualified, whether or not he happens to be white. It is unacceptable to an even greater number that a person who is less accomplished judged by a job-relevant standard be hired, because he is black, in preference to a person who is more accomplished, whatever his race. It is wrong, in their eyes, not because the person who has gained the preference is black but because preferential treatment, regardless of race, is wrong.

Because of the sincerity of their commitment to racial equality, proponents of affirmative action have difficulty acknowledging that opposition to it is based on principle. To understand the liberal defense of affirmative action in the face of this overwhelming opposition, it is necessary to take account of the relation between American racism and the American Creed, as viewed by liberals.

With the rise to prominence of the civil rights movement during the 1950s, followed by the passage of the historic civil rights laws in the middle of the 1960s, Gunnar Myrdal's classic work, *An American Dilemma,* seemed to have won the verdict of history. The American Creed, with its commitment to liberty, equality, and fair play, would prevail. It would prevail because the American dilemma was, ultimately and inescapably, a moral dilemma, and for all the obstacles blocking the way forward, the force of Americans' moral commitments could overcome them. As Myrdal wrote, "America is constantly reaching for . . . democracy at home and abroad. The main trend in its history is the gradual realization of the American Creed."[5] Nothing is foreordained, and an immense effort would be required. Still, through the ultimate authority of America's deepest convictions, "America is free to choose whether the Negro shall remain her liability or become her opportunity."[6]

Under the light of progress, the American Creed presented itself as a force in the service of racial equality. Consistent with this sanguine view, systematic studies of public opinion highlighted the accelerating commitment of white Americans to the principle of racial equality, underscoring a historic transformation of American popular culture. The message of these studies was not blindly celebratory: the persistence of prejudice was documented; so, too, the divisiveness of race as an issue. But the findings gave evidence of a society committed, at its center, to the principle of equality, with race prejudice pushed increasingly toward its fringes. On the available evidence, the American Creed was not merely consistent with the aspiration to racial equality; it was a wellspring of support for it.

The liberalism of the 1970s and 80s has turned the liberalism of the 1950s and 60s on its head.[7] As against Myrdal's view that race bigotry was giving up ground, grudgingly to be sure but steadily all the same, the new view has emphasized the tenacity of prejudice. As against Myrdal's view that racial prejudice drew its strength from an America that increasingly belonged to the past, the new view argues that it remains well-rooted in American values of the present. As against the view that bigotry was being shoved to the periphery of American society, the new view holds that racial prejudice is embedded in its most central institutions. Finally, as against Myrdal's optimism that the American Creed ultimately could and would prevail against race prejudice, the new view holds that those very core values serve as support for racism and ensure its survival.

Distinctions, at least of degree, that used to be drawn—between South and North, or between younger, better-educated, more liberal Americans and older, ill-educated, conservative ones—have gone by the boards. Liberalism has instead invested heavily in the view that race prejudice is bound up with American culture and values and is therefore virulent in the North as well as in the South, among the young as well as among the old, among the best educated as well as among the least. It has, accordingly, tended to see the central tendencies in American life and institutions to be at odds with the needs and feelings of Americans victimized by discrimination and inequality. Rather than presenting itself to the general American public as a representative and advocate of their shared values, liberalism has come to assume the role of the public's critic, and sometimes its adversary.

America, liberalism now maintains, has become two nations. One is black, badly off, and increasingly left to its own devices. The other is white, well-off, and notwithstanding its occasional public professions of good will to black America, indifferent or hostile to those making demands on it. The more evidence that has accumulated on the growth of racial tolerance among whites, the more entrenched has become this image of America racially split into separate nations. As the "separate nations" idea has taken hold, so too has cynicism about whites' expressions of acceptance of blacks. When a public opinion survey shows that the proportion of whites who hold racist sentiments has shrunk dramatically and the proportion who favor the principle of racial equality has grown correspondingly, it is dismissed on the grounds that people are just saying what they think they should say, not what they really think. When study after study demonstrates that a central institution of American society—the school system, for example—promotes racial tolerance, this, too, is dismissed on the grounds that schools just teach whites to say the right thing.

Certainly, there is no shortage of dramatic incidents which seem to serve as inescapable metaphors of a racist America; and as we have shown, the number of whites who remain systematically hostile to blacks is far from trivial. But the pivotal question concerns the fundamental spirit of the times: To what extent is the liberal critique of American popular culture as benign on the surface but unsympathetic and resentful beneath correct? To what extent are white Americans who speak well of black Americans saying not what they think but what they think they should say?

Given the long and murderous history of prejudice and discrimination in America, it is understandable that the burden of proof has been imposed on those who say that white attitudes toward blacks have improved, rather than on those who insist that they haven't. It therefore seemed to us, from the start of our study, that one of the most worthwhile things we could do would be to establish whether there are reasonable grounds for believing that white Americans who say they think well of black Americans mean what they say.

Hence the Excuse Experiments, designed to deliberately provide some whites with a socially acceptable reason to judge a black harshly and to do so in the emotionally charged contexts of crime and welfare. We zeroed in on whites who appear to have consistently positive attitudes toward blacks, reasoning that if, in saying they think well of blacks they are only saying what they think they should say, they should take advantage of the excuse we have handed them to express the negative feelings toward blacks they supposedly harbor. In fact, they do not. In analysis after analysis they give the same weight to damaging information applied to blacks as to whites, no more, no less.

This is, we think, one of the most important results from our study, giving reason to believe that whites who consistently profess good will toward blacks mean what they say. This is not at all to suggest that prejudice has disappeared. On the contrary, we have seen that a substantial number of whites still systematically dislike blacks—describing them in such negative terms as irresponsible, lazy, and violent—and are willing to say so outright to a perfect stranger. Nonetheless, the totality of our results suggests the need to rethink liberalism's critique of the popular culture.

It is necessary to rethink the place of tolerance in American culture partly because the narrowness of the terms in which racial progress has been conceived. Whether on the left or on the right, those who believe progress in racial attitudes has taken place see it in the same terms: the reduction of racial prejudice. But this conception of progress suggests that the issue is only how much ill-will toward blacks remains, with liberals putting the figure higher, conservatives lower. What both liberals and conservatives have overlooked is that not only is there markedly less ill-will toward blacks than there used to be, but there is significantly more good will.

Over the last quarter-century, liberalism has had difficulty mustering faith in the standing of tolerance as a value in American culture. It has, in consequence, put its muscle into coercive policies to achieve racial equality, busing and affirmative action chief among them. These policies, in turn, have evoked anger and resentment on a large scale, and the very vehemence of the popular backlash against them, in an irony of genuinely historical proportions, has served to confirm liberalism in its lack of faith in the larger public's commitment to tolerance. This vicious cycle has tempted liberalism to treat the popular culture as an opposing force to be overcome. It is worth liberalism's serious consideration whether, once again, it wishes to identify itself and its quest for racial progress with the American Creed.

It is also worth liberalism's consideration whether the time has come to modify if not abandon its "two-nations" critique of popular culture—that black and white Americans live "in worlds apart." Granted, this notion is given some credence by current events, such as the disparate reactions of blacks and whites to the O. J. Simpson trial. Yet without at all minimizing the distinct sense of self of blacks or the many divisive issues that keep blacks and whites apart, we believe that our data serve as a reminder that black and white Americans belong to a common culture, not less in what they dispute than in what they honor. We came to this conclusion by focusing precisely on an issue where one would least expect to find consensus— namely, what measure of responsibility blacks themselves bear for the problems they face. The question of responsibility has become intensely controversial in the media, with some commentators pointing to high rates of illegitimacy and crime in the inner cities as evidence of black irresponsibility, and the opponents of these commentators routinely charging them with "blaming the victim." Yet this well-rehearsed controversy notwithstanding, it is the remarkable similarity of blacks' and whites' views on the issue of responsibility, not their dissimilarity, that stands out.

Far and away most black Americans believe that *both* blacks and whites bear responsibility for blacks being worse off. And far and away most white Americans believe the same. Blacks most often select, as the factor responsible for their being worse off, white prejudice and discrimination, but so do whites, if not as often as blacks. The factors that whites most often point to—crime and poor neighborhoods, lack of educational opportunity, problems in the family, a failure of persistence—are the factors blacks point to as well, and just about as often as whites. And the idea that blacks can and should make their way forward without special favors which, when expressed by whites, is taken to be an expression of racism, is just what blacks themselves believe.

In the similarity of their views there is a lesson. Even when blacks and whites turn to the very issue that most deeply divides them—why blacks are still so much worse off than whites—their comments suggest that they largely see the same reality, contested as it is, and what is more, they predominantly share the same standards and values.

■ ■ ■

Is doing more of the same doing enough? Whether viewed from the perspective of black or white Americans, this is the crucial question to consider in the contemporary politics of race. And in weighing an answer, in our view a primary consideration ought to be the growing number of blacks who are, or are at risk of being, immiserated. By every gauge of poverty and disadvantage of which we are aware, the condition of blacks who are badly off is worse now than a generation ago. We are aware that many blacks have also made progress—over the last thirty years the size of the black middle class has roughly tripled—and we are also aware that to say that many blacks now are markedly better off than they used to be is not to say that as yet they are nearly as well-off as whites who are well-off, particularly in terms of wealth.[8] But because of the real progress that has been made, there is now a need to give priority to black Americans who, for whatever reason, failed to catch the wave of rising prosperity and now find themselves at risk of going under.

The balance of opinion on both the political left and right seems in agreement that what is being done on behalf of badly off blacks is not nearly good enough. There is very wide disagreement over what would be best to do, but there is at least as wide agreement that the needs of those who are worst off ought to have a degree of attention paid them that they have not for a decade and more.

It is on the premise that priority now needs to be given to those that are badly off that we want to discuss the merits of a color-blind politics. For a decade and more, arguments in behalf of government efforts to assist blacks have centered on considerations of race. There should be government assistance for blacks, the argument has run, because blacks were so unfairly treated in the past; or because they still are held back by discrimination; or because, as a consequence of past discrimination, they lack the stability of family structure or the network of professional associations or the educational background or the inherited wealth to enjoy a genuinely level playing field. Whatever the specific reason in support of government action to assist blacks, they have shared the ground of race itself as justification.

Our findings call attention to a different course. The very same policy which enjoys the support of only a minority can win the support of a majority if it is advanced in racially inclusive rather than racially restrictive terms. It is more popular to attempt to try to help those who are poor, whether they are black or white, than to try to help just the poor who are also black. What is as important is why this is so. Until now, the argument has been that the way to build support for policies to help the truly disadvantaged and thereby break out of the present impasse over race is to expand the circle of beneficiaries of social welfare policies.[9] The idea is that whites will resist supporting policies targeting blacks because whites cannot benefit from them. This view of the politics of inequality puts at the center a zero-sum calculation of winners and losers, and proposes by way of remedy a biracial coalition on the basis of interests common to both poor blacks and poor whites.

As against this view, which centers on interests common to poor blacks and whites, we have become persuaded of another, which focuses on principles common to blacks and whites whether poor or not. We have made our way to this new view, however obvious it seems to us now, a step at a time. The first was to discover why, if white Americans have a choice between helping blacks who are poor versus helping those who are poor, both blacks and whites, they are markedly more likely to support the racially inclusive rather than a racially restrictive policy. As the School Tax Experiment demonstrated, contrary to the view of many on the left, it had little to do with racism. As important, contrary to the view of others, it had nothing noticeably to do with economic disadvantage. Both findings matter, but for us the second was eye-opening. It meant that, contrary to one of the most influential lines of argument on the left, that of William Julius Wilson, the advantage of moving to a race-neutral politics did not follow from its facilitating a coalition of badly off or economically anxious whites and blacks. On the contrary, policies aimed at helping those who are badly off win more support if they are racially inclusive rather than racially restrictive because they win the support of whites who are well off as well as those who are badly off.

It is not a small point, if the objective is to put together a winning coalition to assist the badly off, black as well as white, that the support of whites, well-off as well as badly-off, can be won by reaching beyond race. And it offers yet another reminder that the fulcrum of liberal politics in America has not been class interest but political principle. In choosing up sides on policies to assist those who are badly off, what counts for ordinary Americans both black and white is not so much who is going to get what as who *should* get what. The second step in our working out a new view was thus to recognize that there is an absolute need to distinguish between the beneficiaries of a policy, and whether they are racially specific or racially neutral, and the justifications for the policy, and whether they are racially specific or racially neutral.

Politics, at its core, is about arguments—about the justifications advanced for a policy, about the criticisms leveled against it. And all arguments are not equal. As our results have shown in a variety of ways, arguments that reach beyond race carry more weight, persuade more people, than those that restrict themselves to the grounds of race. We are not suggesting that the argument that the larger society has a special obligation to make up for injustices done to blacks in the past has lost all its power; still less are we arguing that to make the case for some policies on racially neutral grounds is to foreswear ever advancing any arguments for other policies on racially specific grounds. But we are saying flat-out that the practice of racializing arguments over justice for the last generation has been a godsend for demagogues, black and white.

We are also saying that morally universalistic arguments do—and, it seems to us, should—trump arguments that are morally particularistic.

It would be helpful to remember what we once knew. There are deeper moral considerations, having nothing intrinsically to do with race, that are responsible for the very fact that the issue of race has a moral claim upon us. Two of them are the values of equal opportunity and of equal treatment. It is by appealing to them that more support can be won in behalf of policies to assist the badly off.

The power of these arguments is limited, we recognize. To say that a government poverty program will reach out to assist those who are poor regardless of race is not a good argument to those who start from the premise that government poverty programs are not effective. Nor should it be. But it can be an effective argument to those who are open to argument, either because they are politically in the middle of the road or because they are actually sympathetic to the idea of government activism in behalf of the disadvantaged. The left will not win the support of those on its own side, let alone those in the middle, if it restricts itself to race-specific arguments.

We believe, but have not tried to demonstrate, that a new effort to relieve inequality is necessary. We believe, and have tried to demonstrate, that if liberalism is to lead such an effort, it must restore its standing as a public philosophy. Given the inevitable swing of the political pendulum, it will regain political influence. What is less certain is whether, when liberalism is next ascendant, it will again address the issue of race with all the force of the moral principles of the American Creed behind it.

NOTE ON THE SURVEYS

National Election Study

The National Election Study (NES), funded by the National Science Foundation, is conducted at the Center for Political Studies at the University of Michigan, Ann Arbor. The target population for the study is all voting age adults residing in the contiguous United States, exclusive of individuals living on military bases. The data on public opinion on affirmative action policies in college admission and jobs rely on the 1986, 1988, 1990, 1992, and 1994 NES surveys; the remainder of the data are from the 1992 NES. The number of respondents in each survey were 2,176 (1986), 2,040 (1988), 2,000 (1990), 2,485 (1992), and 1,795 (1994).

QUESTION WORDING: PREJUDICE

"Now I have some questions about different groups in our society. I'm going to show you a seven-point scale on which the characteristics of the people in a group can be rated. Where would you rate (whites/blacks) in general on this scale? (1) Hard-working vs. Lazy (1 = Hard-working, 7 = Lazy); (2) Intelligent vs. Unintelligent (1 = Intelligent, 7 = Unintelligent); (3) Peaceful vs. Violent (1 = Peaceful, 7 = Violent)."

The racial prejudice index was constructed by first subtracting respondents' scores for whites from their scores for blacks and then summing these differences so that higher scores represent greater prejudice toward blacks relative to whites.

QUESTION WORDING: POLITICAL ATTITUDES

Ideology: "We hear a lot of talk these days about liberals and conservatives. Here is a 7-point scale on which the political views that people might hold are arranged from extremely liberal to extremely conservative. Where would you place yourself on this scale, or haven't you thought much about this? [Those who responded 'haven't thought much' were excluded from the analysis.] 1 = Extremely liberal; 2 = Liberal; 3 = Slightly liberal; 4 = Moderate, middle of road; 5 = Slightly conservative; 6 = Conservative; 7 = Extremely conservative." [When trichotomized, it is coded as follows: 1 = Liberal (1-3 in the original scale); 2 = Moderate (4); 3 = Conservative (5-7).]

Party identification: "Generally speaking, do you usually think of yourself as a Democrat, a Republican, an Independent, or what? [If Democrat:] Would you call yourself a strong Democrat or a not very strong Democrat? [If Republican:] Would you call yourself a strong Republican or a not very strong Republican? [If Independent:] Do you think of yourself as closer to the Democratic party or closer to the Republican party? [Some reiterated 'Independent.']"

Preference in admissions to universities for blacks (1986b; 1990; 1992; 1994): "Some people say that because of past discrimination, an extra effort should be made to make sure that qualified blacks are considered for university admission. Others say that this extra effort is wrong because it gives blacks advantages they haven't earned. How do you feel? Are you in favor of or opposed to making an extra effort to make sure qualified blacks are considered for admission to colleges and universities?"

Preference in admissions to universities for blacks (1986a; 1988): "Some people say that because of past discrimination, an extra effort should be made to make sure that qualified blacks are considered for university admission. Others say that this extra effort is wrong because it discriminates against whites. How do you feel? Are you in favor of or opposed to making an extra effort to make sure qualified blacks are considered for admission to colleges and universities?"

Preference in hiring for blacks: "Some people say that because of past discrimination black should be given preference in hiring and promotion. Others say that such preference in hiring and promotion of blacks is wrong because it gives blacks advantage they haven't earned. What about your opinion—are you for or against preferential hiring and promotion for blacks?"

Government efforts to help blacks: "Some people feel that the government in Washington should make every effort to improve the social and economic position of blacks. Others feel that the government should not make any special effort to help blacks because they should help themselves. How do you feel? 1 = Blacks should help themselves; 7 = Government should help blacks."

Government spending to help blacks: "Should federal spending on programs that assist blacks be increased, decreased, or kept about the same?"

Welfare spending: "Should federal spending on welfare programs be increased, decreased, or kept about the same?"

Integration: "Some people say that the government in Washington should see to it that white and black children go to the same schools. Others claim that this is not the government's business. Do you think the government in Washington should see to it that white and black children go to the same schools or stay out of this area as it is not the government's business?"

General Social Survey

The General Social Survey (GSS) has been conducted during February, March, and April of most years from 1972 to 1996. Each survey is an independently drawn sample of English-speaking persons 18 years of age or over who live in noninstitutional arrangements in the United States. The surveys were conducted by the National Opinion Research Center at the University of Chicago.

While these data present an excellent time-series, there are also some questions that are asked in only one survey. Starting in 1985, the GSS has included annual topical modules—groups of questions that focus on a specific topic. In 1990 the focus of that module was race relations. The 1990 GSS is also the only year that contains the questions used to construct the measure of race prejudice. The number of respondents to the 1990 GSS was 1,372.

QUESTION WORDING: PREJUDICE

"Now I have some questions about different groups in our society. I'm going to show you a seven-point scale on which the characteristics of the people in a group can be rated. Where would you rate (whites/blacks) in general on this scale? (1) Hard-working vs. Lazy (1

= Hard-working, 7 = Lazy); (2) Intelligent vs. Unintelligent (1 = Intelligent, 7 = Unintelligent); (3) Peaceful vs. Violent (1 = Peaceful, 7 = Violent)."

QUESTION WORDING: POLITICAL ATTITUDES

Ideology: "We hear a lot of talk these days about liberals and conservatives. Here is a 7-point scale on which the political views that people might hold are arranged from extremely liberal to extremely conservative. Where would you place yourself on this scale, or haven't you thought much about this? [Those who responded 'haven't thought much' were excluded from the analysis.] 1 = Extremely liberal; 2 = Liberal; 3 = Slightly liberal; 4 = Moderate, middle of road; 5 = Slightly conservative; 6 = Conservative; 7 = Extremely conservative." When trichotomized, it is coded as follows: 1 = Liberal (1-3 in the original scale); 2 = Moderate (4); 3 = Conservative (5-7).

Party identification: "Generally speaking, do you usually think of yourself as a Democrat, a Republican, an Independent, or what? [If Democrat:] Would you call yourself a strong Democrat or a not very strong Democrat? [If Republican:] Would you call yourself a strong Republican or a not very strong Republican? [If Independent:] Do you think of yourself as closer to the Democratic party or closer to the Republican party? [Some reiterated 'Independent.']"

Spending to help blacks: "Are we spending too much, too little, or about the right amount on improving the conditions of blacks?"

Government responsibility to help blacks: "Some people think that blacks have been discriminated against for so long that the government has a special obligation to help improve their living standards. Others believe that the government should not be giving special treatment to blacks. Where would you place yourself on this scale? 1 = No special treatment for blacks; 3 = Agree with both answers; 5 = Government is obligated to help blacks."

Race and Politics Study

The Race and Politics Study (RAP), funded by the National Science Foundation, was carried out in 1991 on a nationwide random-digit telephone sample by the Survey Research Center at the University of California, Berkeley. The target population for the study is all English-speaking adults, 18 years of age or older, residing in households with telephones, within the 48 contiguous states. There were 2,223 interviews completed, with a 65.3% response rate.

Because the telephone interviews were computer-assisted, we were able to randomize many elements of the questionnaire. The interviewing was implemented using the CASES software developed by the Computer-Assisted Survey Methods Program of the University of California, Berkeley. When an experimental question was asked, the respondent would be randomly assigned to one of the different conditions. For example, if there were two different versions of a question, approximately one half of the respondents would be asked the first version, while the other half of the respondents would be asked the second version.

QUESTION WORDING: RACIAL STEREOTYPES

The racial prejudice index was created by summing respondents' scores on the following five stereotypes of blacks:

Aggressive/Violent: "How about 'aggressive or violent'? On a scale of 0 to 10, how well do you think it describes most blacks? 1 = Disagree (0-4); 2 = Neutral (5); 3 = Agree (6-10)."

Lazy: "How about 'lazy'? On a scale of 0 to 10, how well do you think it describes most blacks?"

Boastful: "How about 'boastful'? On a scale of 0 to 10, how well do you think it describes most blacks?"

Irresponsible: "How about 'irresponsible'? On a scale of 0 to 10, how well do you think it describes most blacks?"

Complaining: "How about 'complaining'? On a scale of 0 to 10, how well do you think it describes most blacks?"

QUESTION WORDING: POLITICAL ATTITUDES

Ideology: "Generally speaking would you consider yourself to be a liberal, a conservative, a moderate, or haven't you thought much about this? [Those who responded 'haven't thought much' were excluded from the analysis.] [If Liberal:] Do you think of yourself as a strong liberal or a not very strong liberal? [If Conservative:] Do you think of yourself as a strong conservative or a not very strong conservative? [If Moderate:] Do you think of yourself as more like a liberal or more like a conservative? [Some respondents reiterated 'Moderate.']"

Party identification: "Generally speaking, do you usually think of yourself as a Democrat, a Republican, an Independent, or what? [If Democrat:] Would you call yourself a strong Democrat or a not very strong Democrat? [If Republican:] Would you call yourself a strong Republican or a not very strong Republican? [If Independent:] Do you think of yourself as closer to the Democratic Party or closer to the Republican Party? [Some respondents reiterated 'Independent.']"

Two Meanings of Affirmative Action Experiment: "[Version 1a:] Some people say that because of past discrimination, qualified blacks should be given preference in university admissions. Others say that this extra effort is wrong because it discriminates against whites. How do you feel? Are you in favor of or opposed to giving qualified blacks preference in admission to colleges and universities? [Version 1b:] Some people say that because of past discrimination, an extra effort should be made to make sure that qualified blacks are considered for university admission. Others say that this extra effort is wrong because it discriminates against whites. How do you feel? Are you in favor of or opposed to making an extra effort to make sure qualified blacks are considered for admission to colleges and universities?"

Justification for Job Quotas Experiment: "[Version 1a blank.] [Version 1b:] There are some companies where blacks are underrepresented. Do you think that large companies should be required to give a certain number of jobs to blacks, or should the government stay out of this? [Version 1c:] There are some large companies with employment policies that discriminate against blacks. Do you think these large companies should be required to give a certain number of jobs to blacks, or should the government stay out of this?"

Special advantages in jobs and schools: "How about giving blacks and other minorities special advantages in jobs and schools? On a scale from 0 to 10, how much does this anger you?"

List Experiment: "Now I'm going to read you (three/four) things that sometimes make people angry or upset. After I read all (three/four), just tell me how many of them upset you. I don't want to know which ones, just how many. [Version 1a:] The federal government increasing the tax on gasoline; professional athletes getting million-dollar-plus salaries; large corporations polluting the environment. [Version 1b:] The federal government increasing the tax on gasoline; professional athletes getting million-dollar-plus salaries; large corporations polluting the environment; a black family moving next door to you. [Version 1c:] The federal government increasing the tax on gasoline; professional athletes getting million-dollar-plus salaries;

large corporations polluting the environment; black leaders asking the government for affirmative action."

Excuse Experiment, Police Drug Search: "Now consider an instance where the police see two young [Version 1a:] white men about 20 years old. [Version 1b:] black men about 20 years old. [Version 2a:] They are well-dressed and well-behaved, [Version 2b:] They are using foul language, and walking very near a house where the police know drugs are being sold. The police search them and find that they are carrying drugs. Do you think that this is definitely a reasonable search, probably a reasonable search, probably not a reasonable search, or definitely not a reasonable search."

Excuse Experiment, Welfare Mother: "Now think about a [Version 1a:] black woman in her early thirties. [Version 1b:] white woman in her early thirties. [Version 2a:] She is a high school drop out, [Version 2b:] She is a high school graduate, with a ten-year-old child and she has been on welfare for the past year. How likely do you think it is that she will really try hard to find a job in the next year—very likely, somewhat likely, somewhat unlikely, not at all likely."

Government spending for programs to help blacks get more jobs: "Some people feel that the government in Washington should increase spending for programs to help blacks get more jobs. Others feel that blacks should take care of their own problems. How do you feel? Do you think the government should do more or do you feel blacks should rely only on themselves?"

Fight discrimination against blacks in jobs: "Some people feel that the government in Washington should do more to make sure that blacks are not discriminated against in getting jobs. Others feel that blacks should take care of their own problems. How do you feel? Do you think the government should do more or do you feel blacks should rely only on themselves?"

Welfare spending: "Suppose you had a say in making up the federal budget, would you prefer to see more spent, less spent, or the same amount of money spent on welfare as it has been?"

No medical insurance for unemployed: "How about the lack of affordable medical care for people who don't have jobs? On a scale from 0 to 10, how much does this anger you?"

Repeal tax breaks for the rich: "How about special benefits like tax breaks going to the richest people and biggest businesses? On a scale from 0 to 10, how much does this anger you?"

Spend more to reduce unemployment: "How about more money being spent to reduce unemployment? Are you strongly in favor, somewhat in favor, somewhat opposed, or strongly opposed?"

Narrow gap between rich and poor: "How about narrowing the gap in income between the rich and the poor? Are you strongly in favor, somewhat in favor, somewhat opposed, or strongly opposed to these programs?"

Allow abortion: "How about allowing a woman to get an abortion if she wants one? Are you strongly in favor, somewhat in favor, somewhat opposed or strongly opposed to that?"

Not allow prayer in schools: "How about allowing students in public schools to pray or otherwise observe their religion? Are you strongly in favor, somewhat in favor, somewhat opposed, or strongly opposed to that?"

Government Dependency Experiment: "Most [Version 1a:] poor people [Version 1b:] blacks [Version 1c:] poor blacks these days would rather take assistance from the government than make it on their own through hard work. Do you agree strongly, disagree strongly, disagree somewhat, or disagree strongly?"

Integration Experiment: "And how do you feel about [Version 1a:] programs set up by religious and business groups that [Version 1b:] government subsidized housing to [Version 1c:] the government putting its weight behind programs to encourage blacks to buy homes in white suburbs? Are you strongly in favor, somewhat in favor, somewhat opposed, or strongly opposed to that?"

School Tax Experiment: "How do you feel? would you be willing to have your taxes raised a little in order to improve [Version 1:] education in public schools? [Version 2:] educational opportunities for minorities?

Helping Hand Experiment: "Now let's talk about programs to provide [Version 1a:] job training to help people, many of whom are [Version 1b:] welfare to help people, many of whom are [Version 2a:] blacks and minorities who have problems with poverty [Version 2b:] new immigrants from Europe who have problems with poverty. The programs I'm talking about are specially designed to help [Version 3a:] people who have shown that they want to work their way out of their own problems. [Version 3b:] people who have had trouble hanging on to jobs. Are you strongly in favor, somewhat in favor, somewhat opposed, or strongly opposed to these programs?"

1994 Multiple Investigator Study

The Multiple Investigator Study, funded by the National Science Foundation, was carried out from June 15, 1994, through November 4, 1994, on a nationwide random-digit telephone sample by the Survey Research Center at the University of California, Berkeley. The target population for the study is all English-speaking adults, 18 years of age or older, residing in households with telephones, within the 48 contiguous states. There were 1,464 cases, with a response rate of 65.5 percent

Once again, the telephone interviews were computer-assisted, allowing us to randomize many elements of the questionnaire. The interviewing was implemented using the CASES software developed by the Computer-Assisted Survey Methods Program of the University of California, Berkeley.

QUESTION WORDING: POLITICAL ATTITUDES

Ideology: "Generally speaking, would you consider yourself to be a liberal, a conservative, a moderate, or haven't you thought much about this? [Those who responded 'haven't thought much' were excluded from the analysis.] [If Liberal:] Do you think of yourself as a strong liberal or a not very strong liberal? [If Conservative:] Do you think of yourself as a strong conservative or a not very strong conservative? [If Moderate:] Do you think of yourself as more like a liberal or more like a conservative? [Some respondents reiterated 'Moderate.']"

List Experiment: "Now I'm going to read you (four/five) things that sometimes make people angry or upset. After I read all (four/five), just tell me how many of them upset you. I don't want to know which ones, just how many. [Version 1a:] The federal government increasing the tax on gasoline; professional athletes getting million-dollar-plus salaries; requiring seat belts be used when driving; polluting the environment. [Version 1b:] The federal government increasing the tax on gasoline; professional athletes getting million-dollar-plus salaries; requiring seat belts be used when driving; corporations polluting the environment; a black family moving next door to you. [Version 1c:] The federal government increasing the tax on gasoline; professional athletes getting million-dollar-plus salaries; requiring seat belts be used when driving; corporations polluting the environment; black leaders asking the government for affirmative action. [Version 1d:] The federal government increasing the tax on gasoline; professional athletes getting million-dollar-plus salaries; requiring seat belts be used when driving; corporations polluting the environment; inter-racial dating with black teenagers taking out white teenagers. [Version 1e:] The federal government increasing the tax on gasoline; pro-fessional athletes getting million-dollar-plus salaries; requiring seat belts be used when driving; corporations polluting the environment; awarding college scholarships on the basis of race."

Regardless of Race Experiment: "As you may know, unemployment among blacks is high. Some people believe that the government in Washington should be responsible for providing job training to them [Version 1a:] because of the historic injustices blacks have suffered. Other people believe that the government is basically doing as much as it can and that now it is up to blacks to take care of their own problems. [Version 1b:] not because they're black but because the government ought to help people who are out of work and want to find a job whether they're white or black. Other people believe that the government is basically doing as much as it can and that it is now up to people, white or black, to take care of their own problems. If you had to choose, would you say it is mostly the responsibility of the government to provide job training for blacks, or is it mostly up to blacks to take care of their own problems?

Color-Blind Experiment: "Some people believe that the federal gov-ernment in Washington should be responsible for improving the social and economic conditions of [Version 1a:]blacks who are born into poverty. They say that because of the continuing legacy of slavery and discrimination we have a special obligation to help blacks get ahead. [Version 1b:] people who are born into poverty. They say that we ought to try to make sure that everyone has an equal oppor-tunity to succeed. [Version 1c:] blacks who are born into poverty. They say that we ought to try to make sure that everyone has an equal opportunity to succeed. Other people believe that the strength of the American way of life is that people should deal with their problems on their own. If you had to choose, would you say the gov-ernment should take responsibility, or should the government stay out of it?

Overt measures of anger: "Now I'm going to ask you about another thing that sometimes makes people angry or upset. [Version 1a:] Would you feel angry or upset if a black family moved in next door to you? [Version 1b:] Do you get angry or upset when black leaders ask the government for affirmative action? [Version 1c:] Do you get angry or upset about interracial dating with black teenagers taking out white teenagers? [Version 1d:] Do you get angry or upset about awarding college scholarships on the basis of race?"

Commitment to racial harmony and equality: "There are certain issues that everyone agrees are important. For these next questions, I will read you two statements at a time and then I'd like you to tell me which one is more important to you personally. Do you think it is more important to promote traditional religious values in politics and society, or to promote racial harmony and equality between blacks and whites? Do you think it is more important to maintain pride and respect for your country, or to promote racial harmony and equality between blacks and whites?

NOTES

1. Tangled Politics

1. For the most recent and comprehensive reviews, see Gerald David Jaynes and Robin M. Williams Jr., eds., *A Common Destiny: Blacks and American Society* (Washington, D.C.: National Academy Press, 1989). See also Douglas S. Massey and Nancy A. Denton, *American Apartheid: Segregation and the Making of the Underclass* (Cambridge: Harvard University Press, 1993); Melvin L. Oliver and Thomas M. Shapiro, *Black Wealth/White Wealth: A New Perspective on Racial Inequality* (London: Routledge, 1995); Christopher Jencks and Paul E. Peterson, eds., *The Urban Underclass* (Washington, D.C.: Brookings Institution, 1991); William Julius Wilson, *The Truly Disadvantaged: The Inner City, the Underclass, and Public Policy* (Chicago: University of Chicago Press, 1987); and Jennifer L. Hochschild, *Facing Up to the American Dream* (Princeton: Princeton University Press, 1995). For a pioneering analysis of the growing class differences among black Americans, see Michael Hout, "Occupational Mobility of Black Men: 1962 to 1973," *American Sociological Review* 49 (1984): 308–322.

2. For example, it has been argued, most forcefully by Jennifer Hochschild, that if busing to achieve school desegregation and racial equality fails, it will be because of the limits imposed on busing, particularly the decision not to bus on a metropolitan area basis, not because of inherent limits in busing itself. See Jennifer L. Hochschild, *The New American Dilemma: Liberal Democracy and School Desegregation* (New Haven: Yale University Press, 1984).

3. In saying it is not necessary to change public opinion to make

political change possible, we are of course not saying that it is not desirable to change it.

4. Paul M. Sniderman and Thomas Piazza, *The Scar of Race* (Cambridge: Harvard University Press, 1993), sets out the different forms the politics of race now assumes, contrasting three agendas: social welfare, equal treatment, and race-consciousness.

5. The most prominent example is Andrew Hacker. See Andrew Hacker, *Two Nations: Black and White, Separate, Hostile, Unequal* (New York: Vintage, 1992).

6. For a history of the development of the field, see Paul M. Sniderman and Douglas Grob, "Innovations in Experimental Design in General Population Attitude Surveys," in *Annual Review of Sociology,* ed. John Hagan and Karen S. Cook (Palo Alto: Annual Reviews, 1996).

2. Affirmative Action's Vortex

1. In their the first decade of research, the proponents of the symbolic racism argument literally took opposition to affirmative action to be, in and of itself, a measure of racism. In response to criticism, they have acknowledged their error. See Paul M. Sniderman and Philip E. Tetlock, "Symbolic Racism: Problems of Motive Attribution in Political Analysis," *Journal of Social Issues* 42 (1986): 173–187. David O. Sears, "Symbolic Racism," in *Eliminating Racism: Profiles in Controversy,* ed. Phyllis A. Katz and Dalmas A. Taylor (New York: Plenum Press, 1988).

2. Kenneth S. Tollett, "Racism and Race-Conscious Remedies," *American Prospect,* Spring 1990, pp. 91–94.

3. The key pieces in the symbolic racism research program are: David O. Sears and Donald R. Kinder, "Racial Tensions and Voting Behavior in Los Angeles," in *Los Angeles: Viability and Prospects for Metropolitan Leadership,* ed. W. Z. Hirsch (New York: Praeger, 1971); Donald R. Kinder and David O. Sears, "Prejudice and Politics: Symbolic Racism Versus Racial Threats to the Good Life," *Journal of Personality and Social Psychology* 40 (1981): 414–431; John B. McConahay, "Modern Racism, Ambivalence and the Modern Racism Scale," in *Prejudice, Discrimination, Discrimination, and Racism,* ed. John F. Dovidio and Samuel L. Gaertner (Orlando: Academic Press, 1986), pp. 91–125; John B. McConahay and Joseph C. Hough, Jr., "Symbolic Racism," *Journal of Social Issues* 32 (1976):

23–45; and Sears, "Symbolic Racism," in *Eliminating Racism*, ed. Katz and Taylor.

4. The foremost proponent of the group interest hypothesis is Lawrence Bobo. See Lawrence Bobo, "Whites' Opposition to Busing: Symbolic Racism or Realistic Group Conflict?" *Journal of Personality and Social Psychology* 45 (1983): 1196–1210; "Group Conflict, Prejudice, and the Paradox of Contemporary Racial Attitudes," in *Eliminating Racism*, ed. Katz and Taylor; and Lawrence Bobo and James R. Kleugel, "Opposition to Race-Targeting: Self-Interest, Stratification Ideology, or Racial Attitudes," *American Sociological Review* 58 (1993): 443–464.

5. For an enlightening exposition of the problem of concealment, both in general and in the case of affirmative action, see Timur Kuran, *Private Truths, Public Lies: The Social Consequences of Preference Falsification* (Cambridge: Harvard University Press, 1995).

6. The classically comprehensive account is Gordon W. Allport, *The Nature of Prejudice* (Reading, Mass.: Addison-Wesley, 1954). For a first-class effort at a synoptic review of subsequent research, see John Duckitt, *The Social Psychology of Prejudice* (New York: Praeger, 1992).

7. Operationally, a seven-point scale anchored at opposing ends by contrasting adjectives was used.

8. The items, equally weighted, were summed.

9. Figure 1 is based on a logistic regression analysis in which racial prejudice is used to predict opposition to affirmative action. Logistic regression is used rather than the ordinary least squares model because the dependent variable is dichotomous. Moreover, the logit coefficients, unlike the standard correlation coefficients, are not constrained by ceiling effects imposed by skewed marginals.

10. Calculating the relation at the zero order, it is worth observing, credits the influence of any other factor correlated with racial prejudice to racial prejudice, thus favoring an over-estimate of the relation between prejudice and opposition to affirmative action.

11. We have found two works particularly insightful, and want to acknowledge their assistance, not only at this juncture but throughout: Hugh Davis Graham, *The Civil Rights Era: Origins and Development of National Policy* (New York: Oxford Univer-

sity Press, 1990), and Andrew Kull, *The Color-Blind Constitution* (Cambridge: Harvard University Press, 1992).

12. Quoted by Kull, *The Color-Blind Constitution*, p. 200.

13. The corollary right—that whites could not be disadvantaged for being white—was explicitly affirmed by the floor managers of the 1964 Civil Rights bill both in debate and in interpretative memoranda and spelled out in Title VII of the 1964 Civil Rights Law. In addition, a clarifying amendment was inserted into the text of the law itself stating: "Nothing contained in this title shall be interpreted to require any employer . . . to grant preferential treatment to any individual or to any group because of the race . . . of such individual or to any group because on an account of an imbalance which may exist with respect to the total number of percentage of persons of any race . . . employed by any employer . . . in comparison with the total number or percentage of persons of such race . . . in any community . . . or in the available work force in any community . . ." Kull, *The Color-Blind Constitution*, pp. 202–203. See also Graham, *The Civil Rights Era*.

14. The principal investigator of the study was Professor William L. Miller, Edward Caird Professor of Politics at the University of Glasgow. Professor Miller generously invited suggestions for experiments, and we thank him for use of these results. For an initial report on the British Study, see William L. Miller, ed., *Alternatives to Freedom* (London: Longman, 1995). For a full report, see William L. Miller, Annie May Timpson, and Michael Lessnoff, *Political Culture in Contemporary Britain* (Oxford: Oxford University Press, 1996).

15. In all, the experiment had six conditions: whether the law should require [large private companies\the government and civil service] to hire a fixed percentage of [women\Blacks and Asians\disabled people], or should [women\Blacks and Asians\disabled people] get no special attention. See Miller, *Alternatives to Freedom*.

16. A third conclusion can also be drawn from the British results. Since opposition to quotas in private industry is as common as in the public domain, it cannot be rooted in specific beliefs about what government distinctively should, or should not, be authorized to do.

17. The reasoning is strategic, as Alfred Blumrosen, an early official

of the Equal Employment Opportunity Commission, observed. To deal with the problems of housing, education, and the like for blacks would not yield a payoff quickly enough. But if discrimination was broadly defined as "all conduct which adversely affects minority group employment opportunities, the prospects for rapid improvement in minority employment opportunities are greatly increased." Quoted in Terry Eastland, *Ending Affirmative Action: The Case for Colorblind Justice* (New York: Basic Books, 1996), p. 46.

18. For the original presentation of the results, see Sniderman and Piazza, *The Scar of Race.*

19. Affirmative action, in the sense of preferential treatment and racial quotas, was introduced under the so-called Philadelphia Plan by Richard Nixon, acting at the request of George Schultz, in an effort to integrate construction unions, which had notoriously excluded Blacks from apprenticeships, and thereby membership. See Graham, *The Civil Rights Era.* For an account of the role of race in reshaping the American party system, see Edward G. Carmines and James A. Stimson, *Issue Evolution: Race and the Transformation of American Politics* (Princeton: Princeton University Press, 1989).

20. The person primarily responsible for conceiving and developing the "list" procedure for the study of racial attitudes is our colleague Professor James Kuklinski. For more information on the procedure, see James H. Kuklinski, Paul M. Sniderman, Kathleen Knight, Thomas Piazza, Philip E. Tetlock, Gordon R. Lawrence, and Barbara Mellers, "Racial Prejudice and Attitudes toward Affirmative Action," *American Journal of Political Science,* in press.

21. This assumes, of course, that he doesn't say that all of the items make him angry. In the development of the measures, we attempted to minimize the risk of this by working to achieve a mean in the baseline condition of about 2. We succeeded in this, but not in minimizing the variance, and this is one reason for the subsequent replication of the List Experiment.

22. For maximum validity, the measure of liberalism-conservatism is the standard self-identification measure.

23. These studies were conducted in the first round of the Multiple Investigator Project. The Multiple Investigator, funded by the National Science Foundation, is a new facility providing a com-

mon platform to research teams across the country to conduct independently designed studies.

24. Specifically, the fourth item read: "requiring seat belts be used when driving." It is worth emphasizing that through pretesting we assured that the mean scores of the baseline condition remained under 2.

25. Specifically, the mean in the baseline condition, for whites, was 2.23; and only 7 percent scored 4 on it, effectively eliminating misleading ceiling effects.

26. Note that the randomized operators are constrained to avoid respondents who have been asked an overt item from being assigned to the same item in a covert treatment. See Martin Gilens, Paul M. Sniderman, and James H. Kuklinski, "Affirmative Action and the Politics of Realignment" (unpublished, 1996).

27. It is worth underlining that the wording for questions were identical in the direct and indirect conditions, guaranteeing that the "increase" in anger observed in the test condition in the List Experiment is based on exactly comparable measures.

28. To obtain the most robust estimates, given the need to compare liberals and conservatives, the n's are increased by combining the two affirmative action conditions. See Gilens, Sniderman, and Kuklinski, "Affirmative Action and the Politics of Realignment."

29. See, for example, Susan D. Clayton and Faye J. Crosby, *Justice, Gender, and Affirmative Action* (Ann Arbor: University of Michigan Press, 1995), p. 5.

30. Bobo and Kleugel, "Opposition to Race-Targeting."

31. For an especially acute and compelling argument in behalf of affirmative action and preferential treatment, see Amy Gutmann, "Responding to Racial Injustice," in K. Anthony Appiah and Amy Gutmann, *Color Conscious: The Political Morality of Race* (Princeton: Princeton University Press, 1996).

32. Guttman, "Responding to Racial Injustice," p. 124.

33. For the most comprehensive statement of this view see Richard D. Kahlenberg, *The Remedy: Class, Race, and Affirmative Action* (New York: Basic Books, 1996).

3. The Power of Prejudice

1. In our 1986 study, reported in *The Scar of Race*, we made our first attempt to measure racial prejudice directly, albeit on a regional

basis. Subsequently, under the leadership of Lawrence Bobo, the General Social Survey introduced in 1990 a direct measure of racial prejudice, key parts of which were used in the 1992 National Election Study.

2. For guidance, we are particularly indebted to Myron Rothbart and Oliver P. John. See, for example, Rothbart and John, "Intergroup Relations and Stereotype Change: A Social-Cognitive Analysis and Some Longitudinal Findings," in *Prejudice, Politics, and the American Dilemma*, ed. Paul M. Sniderman, Philip E. Tetlock, and Edward G. Carmines (Stanford: Stanford University Press, 1993). We have also found very helpful Wallace E. Lambert and Donald M. Taylor, *Coping with Cultural and Racial Diversity in Urban America* (New York: Praeger, 1990).

3. Respondents were given a scale, running from 0 to 10, to indicate how good a description an adjective is of "most blacks," with 0 indicating that it is a very poor description, and 10 a very good one. Since 5 is the neutral point, agreement is defined as a score of 6 or higher.

4. For the classic *Scientific American* series, see Herbert H. Hyman and Paul B. Sheatsley, "Attitudes toward Desegregation," *Scientific American* 195 (1956): 35–39; Herbert H. Hyman and Paul B. Sheatsley, "Attitudes toward Desegregation," *Scientific American* 211 (1964): 16–23; D. Garth Taylor, Paul B. Sheatsley, and Andrew M. Greeley, "Attitudes toward Racial Integration," *Scientific American* 238 (1978): 42–51. For a more recent, exemplary analysis of trends in American racial attitudes, see Howard Schuman, Charlotte Steeh, and Lawrence Bobo, *Racial Attitudes in America: Trends and Interpretations* (Cambridge: Harvard University Press, 1985).

5. For example, see Hacker, *Two Nations*.

6. The dependent variable is measured in two categories, whether they believe it is a reasonable search or not a reasonable search.

7. The two items, equally weighted, are combined, and the overall distribution then trichotomized, with the racially tolerant operationally equalling the upper third.

8. Again, in order to assure a fair test, the items, equally weighted, were summed and the distribution for the overall index trichotomized.

9. The pattern of results, which shows a higher relation between prejudice and social welfare policies, reproduces the findings we originally reported in *The Scar of Race*.

10. For the classic study, see Theodor W. Adorno, Else Frenkel-Brunswick, Daniel J. Levinson, and R. Nevitt Sanford, *The Authoritarian Personality* (New York: Harper, 1950).

11. See, for example, C. Vann Woodward, *American Counterpoint: Slavery and Racism in the North-South Dialogue*, 2nd ed. (Boston: Little, Brown, 1983).

12. See Carmines and Stimson, *Issue Evolution*.

13. This position has most forcefully been argued by Thomas Byrne Edsall and Mary Edsall, *Chain Reaction: The Impact of Race, Rights and Taxes on American Politics* (New York: Norton, 1991); see also Steven M. Gillon, *The Democrats' Dilemma* (New York: Columbia Press, 1992); Peter Brown, *Minority Party* (Washington, D.C.: Regnery Gateway, 1991); and Robert Huckfeldt and Carol Weitzel Kohfeld, *Race and the Decline of Class in American Politics* (Urbana and Chicago: University of Illinois Press, 1989).

14. Figure 12 as well as figures 1 and 2 in the Appendix is based on a logistic regression analysis in which prejudice is used to predict support for racial policies.

15. These counter-arguments are of two kinds—methodological and substantive. We have conducted a number of technical analyses of potential methodological artifacts, such as differential restrictions of range and differential reliability of measurement. Here we concentrate on substantive counter-arguments.

16. The classic study of the lack of consistency in the political belief systems of ordinary citizens is Philip E. Converse, "The Nature of Belief Systems in Mass Publics," in *Ideology and Discontent,* ed. David E. Apter (New York: Free Press, 1964). See also Teresa Levitan and Warren E. Miller, "Ideological Interpretations of Presidential Elections," *American Political Science Review* 73 (1979): 751–771.

17. This special experiment, it is worth pointing out, was located very near the beginning of the interview, before issues of race had been introduced and respondents, by dint of having been run through a series of race-targeted questions, had a chance to practice and smooth out their responses.

18. Four positions were coded: strongly favor; somewhat favor; somewhat oppose; strongly oppose. All respondents were first asked how they feel about blacks buying houses in whites suburbs. Those opposed—about 1 in 10—were not asked whether they favor or oppose a specific method to achieve integration in

this form, since they are opposed as a matter of principle. Analyses show that this missing data raises no problem of bias.

4. Color-Blind Politics

1. David Southern, *Gunnar Myrdal and Black-White Relations: The Use and Abuse of An American Dilemma, 1944–1969* (Baton Rouge: Louisiana State University Press, 1987), pp. 263–264.
2. *Regents of the University of California v. Bakke,* 438 U.S. 265 (1978): 407.
3. See Hacker, *Two Nations.*
4. The contrast in the General Social Survey items, it is worth noting, is inexact, since for all three the comparison is between assistance for those who are black vs. help for those who are poor, whereas logically it should be between those who are black and poor and those who are poor, not those who are black, whether or not they are poor. Still, it is better to work with all the evidence, even though some of it is imperfect, than with only some of it. For the first report on these results, see Bobo and Kluegel, "Opposition to Race-Targeting."
5. Logically, one could argue that this shows that people who say they like blacks really don't. But all the results we have presented on exactly this measure demonstrate that this objection is false: whenever white attitudes toward blacks make a difference, it is always the case that the more favorable whites' attitudes are toward blacks, the more supportive they are of government assistance for blacks.
6. See, for example, Theda Skocpol, "Targeting within Universalism: Politically Viable Policies to Combat Poverty in the United States," in *The Urban Underclass,* ed. Christopher Jencks and Paul E. Peterson (Washington, D.C.: Brookings, 1991).
7. Specifically, the following equation is estimated: $Y=a+x_1+x_2+x_1x_2+u_i$ where x_1=whether the beneficiary is black, x_2=when assistance takes the form of welfare, x_1x_2= the interaction of the two variables.
8. For both liberals and conservatives, when welfare is involved, the interaction between the race of the beneficiary and the issue of individual effort is statistically significant ($p=<.05$), but in precisely the opposite direction, conservatives being more likely to favor help for white immigrants, liberals for blacks.

9. See Bobo and Kluegel, "Opposition to Race-Targeting."

10. The practice of race norming would be morally defensible if it is shown (1) that the test in use is racially biased and (2) that the adjusted scores (after race norming) more closely match applicants' true abilities than their original scores.

11. Gordon W. Allport, *The Nature of Prejudice* (Reading, MA: Addison-Wesley, 1988), p. 276. italics in original.

12. Troy Duster et al., *Diversity Project: Final Report* (Berkeley: Institute for the Study of Social Change, University of California at Berkeley, 1991).

13. Cornel West, *Race Matters* (New York: Vintage Press, 1993), p. 64.

14. The distinction between who and why is analytical: the act of specifying a group to receive assistance—for example, crippled orphans (or, less fancifully, blacks on welfare) can implicitly present a reason for or against assistance.

15. The Regardless of Race Experiment is drawn from the Multiple Investigator Study.

16. Italics added for emphasis.

17. Italics added for emphasis.

18. As a formal test, we specified an interaction term, between the experimental variation and level of information, which fails to meet conventional levels of statistical significance.

19. See, for example, Jaynes and Williams, *A Common Destiny.*

20. See, for example, Ellis Cose, *The Rage of the Privileged Class* (New York: Harper/Perennial, 1993).

21. Henry H. Bauer, *Scientific Literacy and the Myth of the Scientific Method* (Urbana and Chicago: University of Illinois Press, 1992), p. 39.

5. Liberalism's Predicament

1. See, for example, Stephen Steinberg, *Turning Back: The Retreat from Racial Justice in American Thought and Policy* (New York: Beacon, 1996); Manning Marable, *Beyond Black and White: Transforming African-American Politics* (New York: Verso, 1996); bell hooks, *Killing Rage: Ending Racism* (New York: Holt, 1996).

2. The classic source of this argument is Charles Murray, *Losing Ground: American Social Policy, 1950–1980* (New York: Basic Books, 1984).

3. See especially William Julius Wilson, *The Declining Significance of*

Race (Chicago: University of Chicago Press, 1978), and *The Truly Disadvantaged.*

4. For an exceptional work, see Douglas S. Massey and Nancy Denton, *American Apartheid.*

5. Gunnar Myrdal, *An American Dilemma: The Negro Problem and American Democracy* (New York: Harper and Row), p. 1021.

6. Ibid., p. 1022, italics in original.

7. For an intellectual history of changing views on the place of race, see Walter A. Jackson, *Gunnar Myrdal and America's Conscience: Social Engineering and Racial Liberalism, 1938–1987* (Chapel Hill: University of North Carolina Press, 1990). Among the works that have had the most influence on us, we want especially to mention Jim Sleeper, *The Closest of Strangers: Liberalism and the Politics of Race in New York* (New York: Norton, 1990).

8. For an excellent work, see Melvin L. Oliver and Thomas M. Shapiro, *Black Wealth/White Wealth: A New Perspective on Racial Inequality* (New York: Routledge, 1995).

9. Here we were very much influenced by William Julius Wilson's, *The Truly Disadvantaged.*

REFERENCES

Adorno, Theodor W., Else Frenkel-Bruswik, Daniel J. Levinson, and R. Nevitt Sanford. 1950. *The Authoritarian Personality*. New York: Harper.

Allport, Gordon W. 1954. *The Nature of Prejudice*. Reading, MA: Addison-Wesley. Rpt. 1988. Reading, MA: Addison-Wesley.

Bauer, Henry H. 1992. *Scientific Literacy and the Myth of the Scientific Method*. Urbana and Chicago: University of Illinois Press.

Bobo, Lawrence. 1983. "Whites' Opposition to Busing: Symbolic Racism or Realistic Group Conflict?" *Journal of Personality and Social Psychology* 45: 1196–1210.

——— 1988. "Group Conflict, Prejudice, and the Paradox of Contemporary Racial Attitudes." In *Eliminating Racism: Profiles in Controversy*, eds. Phyllis A. Katz and Dalmas A. Taylor. New York: Plenum Press.

Bobo, Lawrence, and James R. Kluegel. 1993. "Opposition to Race-Targeting: Self-Interest, Stratification Ideology, or Racial Attitudes." *American Sociological Review* 58: 443–464.

Brown, Peter. 1991. *Minority Party*. Washington D.C.: Regnery Gateway.

Carmines, Edward G., and James A. Stimson. 1989. *Issue Evolution: Race and the Transformation of American Politics*. Princeton: Princeton University Press.

Clayton, Susan D., and Faye J. Crosby. 1995. *Justice, Gender, and Affirmative Action*. Ann Arbor: University of Michigan Press.

Converse, Philip E. 1964. "The Nature of Belief Systems in Mass Publics." In *Ideology and Discontent*, ed. David E. Apter. New York: Free Press.

Cose, Ellis. 1993. *The Rage of the Privileged Class*. New York: Harper/Perennial.

Duckitt, John. 1992. *The Social Psychology of Prejudice*. New York: Praeger.

Duster, Troy, et. al. 1991. *Diversity Project: Final Report*. Berkeley CA: Institue for Study of Social Change, University of California at Berkeley.

Eastland, Terry. 1996. *Ending Affirmative Action: The Case for Colorblind Justice*. New York: Basic Books.

Edsall, Thomas Byrne, and Mary D. Edsall. 1991. *Chain Reaction: The Impact of Race, Rights, and Taxes on American Politics*. New York: W. W. Norton.

Feagin, Joe, and Melvin P. Sikes. 1994. *Living with Racism: The Black Middle-Class Experience*. Boston: Beacon Press.

Gilens, Martin, Paul M. Sniderman, and James H. Kuklinski. Unpublished, 1996. "Affirmative Action and the Politics of Realignment."

Gillon, Steven M. 1992. *The Democrats' Dilemma*. New York: Columbia Press.

Graham, Hugh Davis. 1990. *The Civil Rights Era: Origins and Development of National Policy*. New York: Oxford University Press.

Gutmann, Amy. 1996. "Responding to Racial Injustice." In K. Anthony Appiah and Amy Gutmann, *Color Conscious: The Political Morality of Race*. Princeton: Princeton University Press.

Hacker, Andrew. 1992. *Two Nations: Black and White, Separate, Hostile, Unequal*. New York: Charles Scribners Sons.

Hochschild, Jennifer L. 1984. *The New American Dilemma: Liberal Democracy and School Desegregation*. New Haven: Yale University Press.

——— 1995. *Facing Up to the American Dream*. Princeton: Princeton University Press.

hooks, bell. 1996. *Killing Rage: Ending Racism*. New York: Holt.

Hout, Michael. 1984. "Occupational Mobility of Black Men: 1962 to 1973." *American Sociological Review* 49:308–322.

Huckfeldt, Robert, and Carol Weitzel Kohfeld. 1989. *Race and the Decline of Class in American Politics*. Urbana and Chicago: University of Illinois Press.

Hyman, Herbert H., and Paul B. Sheatsley. 1956. "Attitudes toward Desegregation." *Scientific American* 195: 35–39.

———— 1964. "Attitudes toward Desegregation." *Scientific American* 211: 16–23.

Jackson, Walter A. 1990. *Gunnar Myrdal and America's Conscience: Social Engineering and Racial Liberalism, 1938–1987.* Chapel Hill: University of North Carolina Press.

Jaynes, Gerald David, and Robin M. Williams Jr., eds. 1989. *A Common Destiny: Blacks and American Society.* Washington, D.C.: National Academy Press.

Jencks, Christopher, and Paul E. Peterson, eds. 1991. *The Urban Underclass.* Washington, D.C.: Brookings Institution.

Kahlenberg, Richard D. 1996. *The Remedy: Class, Race, and Affirmative Action.* New York: Basic Books.

Kinder, Donald R., and David O. Sears. 1981. "Prejudice and Politics: Symbolic Racism Versus Racial Threats to the Good Life." *Journal of Personality and Social Psychology* 40: 414–431.

Kuklinski, James H., Paul M. Sniderman, Kathleen Knight, Thomas Piazza, Philip E. Tetlock, Gordon R. Lawrence, and Barbara Mellers. In Press. "Racial Prejudice and Attitudes toward Affirmative Action." *American Journal of Political Science.*

Kull, Andrew. 1992. *The Color-Blind Constitution.* Cambridge: Harvard University Press.

Kuran, Timur. 1995. *Private Truths, Public Lies: The Social Consequences of Preference Falsification.* Cambridge: Harvard University Press.

Lambert, Wallace E., and Donald M. Taylor. 1990. *Coping with Cultural and Racial Diversity in Urban America.* New York: Praeger.

Levitan, Teresa, and Warren E. Miller. 1979. "Ideological Interpretations of Presidential Elections." *American Political Science Review* 73: 751–771.

Marable, Manning. 1996. *Beyond Black and White: Transforming African-American Politics.* New York: Verso.

Massey, Douglas S., and Nancy A. Denton. 1993. *American Apartheid: Segregation and the Making of the Underclass.* Cambridge: Harvard University Press.

McConahay, John B. 1986. "Modern Racism, Ambivalence, and the Modern Racism Scale." In *Prejudice, Discrimination and Racism: Theory and Research,* eds. John F. Dovidio and Samuel L Gaertner. New York: Academic Press.

McConohay, John B., and Joseph C. Hough, Jr. 1976. "Symbolic Racism." *Journal of Social Issues* 32:23–45.

Miller, William L., ed. 1995. *Alternatives to Freedom: Arguments and Opinions*. London: Longman.

Miller, William, Annie May Timpson, and Michael Lessnoff. 1996. *Political Culture in Contemporary Britain*. Oxford: Oxford University Press.

Murray, Charles. 1984. *Losing Ground: American Social Policy, 1950–1980*. New York: Basic Books.

Myrdal, Gunnar. 1944. *An American Dilemma: The Negro Problem and American Democracy*. New York: Harper and Row.

Oliver, Melvin L., and Thomas M. Shapiro. 1995. *Black Wealth/White Wealth: A New Perspective on Racial Inequality*. New York: Routledge.

Regents of the University of California v. Bakke. 1978. 438 U.S. 265.

Rothrbart, Myron, and Oliver P. John. 1993. "Intergroup Relations and Stereotype Change: A Social-Cognitive Analysis and Some Longitudinal Findings." In *Prejudice, Politics, and the American Dilemma*, eds. Paul M. Sniderman, Philip E. Tetlock, and Edward G. Carmines. Stanford: Stanford University Press.

Schuman, Howard, Charlotte Steeh, and Lawrence Bobo. 1985. *Racial Attitudes in America: Trends and Interpretations*. Cambridge: Harvard University Press.

Sears, David O. 1988. "Symbolic Racism." In *Eliminating Racism: Profiles in Controversy*, eds. Phyllis A. Katz and Dalmas A. Taylor. New York: Plenum Press.

Sears, David O., and Donald R. Kinder. 1971. "Racial Tensions and Voting Behavior in Los Angeles." In *Los Angeles: Viability and Prospects for Metropolitan Leadership*, ed. W.Z. Hirsch. New York: Praeger.

Skocpol, Theda. 1991. "Targeting within Universalism: Politically Viable Policies to Combat Poverty in the United States." In *The Urban Underclass*, eds. Christopher Jencks and Paul E. Peterson. Washington, D.C.: Brookings.

Sleeper, Jim. 1990. *The Closest of Strangers: Liberalism and the Politics of Race in New York*. New York: Norton.

Sniderman, Paul M., and Douglas Grob. 1996. "Innovations in Experimental Design in General Population Attitude Surveys." In *Annual Review of Sociology*, ed. John Hagan and Karen Cook. Palo Alto: Annual Review.

Sniderman, Paul M., and Thomas Piazza. 1993. *The Scar of Race.* Cambridge: Harvard University Press.

Sniderman, Paul M., and Philip E. Tetlock. 1986. "Symbolic Racism: Problems of Motive Attribution in Political Analysis." *Journal of Social Issues* 42:179–187.

Southern, David. 1987. *Gunnar Myrdal and Black-White Relations: The Use and Abuse of An American Dilemma, 1944–1969.* Baton Rouge: Louisiana State University Press.

Steinberg, Stephen. 1996. *Turning Back: The Retreat from Racial Justice in American Thought and Policy.* New York: Beacon. 1996.

Taylor, D. Garth, Paul B. Sheatsley, and Andrew M. Greeley. 1978. "Attitudes toward Racial Integration." *Scientific American* 238: 42–51.

Tollett, Kenneth S. 1990. "Racism and Race-Conscious Remedies." *American Prospect* (Spring) 91–94.

West, Cornel. 1993. *Race Matters.* New York: Vintage Press.

Wilson, William Julius. 1978. *The Declining Significance of Race.* Chicago: University of Chicago Press.

—— 1987. *The Truly Disadvantaged: The Inner City, the Underclass and Public Policy.* Chicago: University of Chicago Press.

—— 1996. *When Work Disappears: The World of the New Urban Poor.* New York: Alfred A. Knopf.

Woodward, C. Vann. 1983. *American Counterpoint: Slavery and Racism in North-South Dialogue,* 2nd ed. Boston: Little, Brown.

■

APPENDIXES

APPENDIX 1
White Support for Government Programs to Help Blacks, by
Ideology, Partisanship, and Level of Prejudice

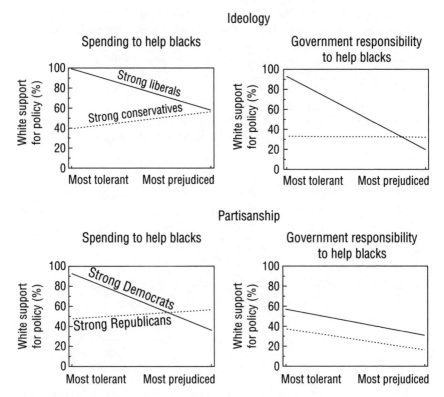

Source: 1990 General Social Survey. Prejudice ranges from most tolerant 1% to the most prejudiced.

APPENDIX 2
White Support for Government Programs to Help Blacks, by Ideology, Partisanship, and Level of Prejudice

Ideology

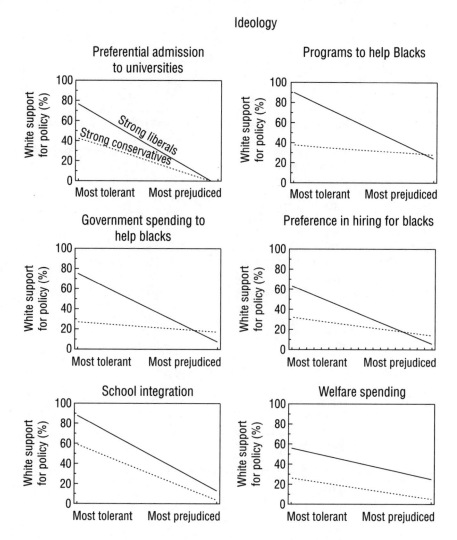

Partisanship

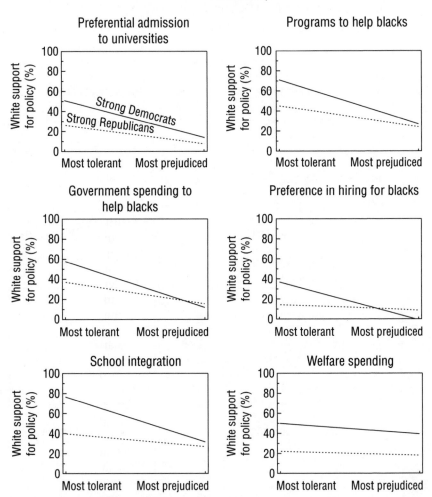

Source: 1992 National Election Study. Prejudice ranges from most tolerant 1% to the most prejudiced 1%.

ACKNOWLEDGMENTS

Publishing a study of public opinion is somewhat like participating in a relay race in which credit goes only to those running the last lap. We want to call attention here to two persons who made indispensable contributions to our research effort from with the very first lap—the design of the study itself. Thomas Piazza, our colleague at the Survey Research Center at the University of California at Berkeley, has been a leader in the development of computer-assisted interviewing techniques, as well as a major player in the design of the Race and Politics Study. Karen Garrett, Field Director of the Survey Research Center, was responsible for working through the final version of the questionnaires of both surveys we carried out, as well as supervising the fieldwork procedure. She has won a national reputation, as researchers who have participated in the Multiple Investigator Surveys will testify, for exactness and imagination in the design of survey instruments.

Other colleagues across the country who have participated in designing the instruments and analyzing the data of the Race and Politics Study are Professors Martin Gilens, Jon Hurwitz, Kathleen Knight, James H. Kuklinski, Mark Peffley, and Laura Stoker. We are grateful for their valuable contributions to this collaborative venture. This study is itself part of a larger collaboration with Philip E. Tetlock, who, on this project as on every other, has been a splendid partner. It has been our exceptional good fortune also to have as a colleague J. Merrill Shanks, Director of the Program in Computer-Assisted Survey Methods at the University of California at Berkeley; the programs for computer-assisted interviewing that he and his colleagues created have been essential to our studies.

For special encouragement and assistance on this project, we want to thank Fern Glover and Lisa Kermish at the Survey Research Center and, at Indiana University, Jeff Layman and William Morgan, who made countless contributions to both the analysis and the argument. We are indebted also to Henry E. Brady, Dana Chabot, Robert Huckfeldt, Jeff Isaac, Robert Rohrschneider, Martin Sanchez-Jankowski, and James A. Wiley, who have taught us, by example, to care more for getting things right than being right. We also want to thank Dr. Arthur J. Lurie for an instructively close, and characteristically generous, reading of the manuscript.

The two national surveys on which this study is based were funded with the support of the Political Science Program at the National Science Foundation (SES-8508937 and SBR93-09946, respectively). We thank the Foundation and Dr. Frank Scioli for the sustained support and encouragement they have extended over the last decade in developing a new approach to survey research. A Fellowship appointment at the Institute for Advanced Study at Indiana University allowed us to work across a desk rather than across the country, and we want particularly to thank the Institute's former Director, Henry H. H. Remak.

At Harvard University Press, Aida Donald provided a mandate for our writing up original research in a way that would be clear to a thoughtful reader. So far as we have succeeded, we have Susan Wallace Boehmer to thank for editorial advice, once again.

It is completely gratuitous, for anyone who knows us, to say that we are onesidedly indebted to our respective partners, Suzie and Ethel.

INDEX